D1476900

THE UNAUTHORIZED HALO® 2 BATTLE GUIDE

Advanced Combat Techniques

Stephen Cawood

SVP, Thomson Course Technology PTR: Andy Shafran

Publisher: Stacy L. Hiquet

Senior Marketing Manager: Sarah O'Donnell

Marketing Manager: Heather Hurley

Manager of Editorial Services: Heather Talbot

Acquisitions Editor: Mitzi Koontz

Senior Editor: Mark Garvey

Associate Marketing Manager: Kristin Eisenzopf

Marketing Coordinator: Jordan Casey

Project Editor: Sandra Wilson

Course Technology PTR Market Coordinator: Elizabeth Furbish

Interior Layout Tech: Bill Hartman

Cover Designer: Mike Tanamachi

Indexer: Katherine Stimson

Proofreader: Sara Gullion

ISBN: 1-59200-700-7

Library of Congress Catalog Card Number: 2004114485

Printed in the United States of America

04 05 06 07 08 BM 10 9 8 7 6 5 4 3 2 1

THOMSON

™

COURSE TECHNOLOGY

Professional ■ Trade ■ Reference

Thomson Course Technology PTR, a division of Thomson Course Technology
25 Thomson Place ■ Boston, MA 02210 ■ http://www.courseptr.com

To my love, Christa.

Special Thanks

I'd like to thank my agent, Neil Salkind (StudioB.com).

Special thanks to Crew 116 and the other Halo experts. I couldn't have done it without your help:

Reed Townsend
DJ Martin
Matt Childerston
Bret Anderson
Theo Michel
Justin Long

I'd also like to thank the following people for their help with the book:

Patrick 'PC' Chin
Rasool Rayani
Mike Laing
Mitzi Koontz
Bill Hartman
Mike Tanamachi
Christa Peters
Bruce Clarke
Michal Piaseczny
Scott Fynn
Chris White

Thanks to the 'Battle Guide Players' who created the screen shots used in this book:

Rasool Rayani
Pat Chin
Christa Peters
And finally, thanks to Bungie and Microsoft for creating the Halo universe.

Table of Contents

Chapter 1 : Introduction

11:00 hours, New Mombasa: Game: Small Team, Single Flag CTF

A Spartan known as 'Armed' spawns on the Zanzibar beach with his small blue team. Armed has played this level often enough to know where all of the weapons are located. Immediately, he hops over a broken wall and hightails it to the Sniper Rifle. On his way, he figures he'll also grab the Battle Rifle. As he approaches a crumbling staircase, he sees that two other blue team members are heading the same way; he reaches the top of the stairwell just in time to see one of them grab his Battle Rifle.

"Ah well, I'll just have some fun picking off the red team from across the map," he thinks to himself as he turns toward the Sniper Rifle. To his horror, the same teammate proceeds to grab the Sniper Rifle as well. "What a jerk," he says out loud and then quickly checks to see if his mike is muted. Fortunately, it is.

Armed's teammate takes off with his favorite weapon.

With no Sniper Rifle, Armed figures he had better head for the Shotgun location. He jumps over the blue sniper—who is now taking aim on the red base—and proceeds toward his favorite weapon. But there is still another blue in front of him. Before he can reach for his mute button, the other blue has acquired his Shotgun.

This time he turns on his mike and yells at his teammate. "What the hell man? What am I supposed to fight with?" The reply comes back immediately over proximity communication, "Dude, relax! This is the first weapon I've taken." Armed is frustrated and can't help but yell back, "Fine, you guys suck. I'm going in with my pea shooter!"

A bad time to attack.

Armed decides that he will go in with his Sub Machine Gun (SMG) and show his teammates what happens when they hoard weapons. As Armed moves down the side of the map, he wonders why he doesn't hear sniper fire or rocket explosions. He asks himself, "What is my useless team doing?"

He looks over to the other side of the map just in time to see a Warthog roar by with the rest of his team. Armed seizes this chance to join his team in a unified assault. He runs toward the side of the base. As he enters, he sees that his team is taking fire. Armed stops in his tracks. The team indicators now show red Xs. They're not taking fire; they're dead. Armed decides that he's already close to the base so he may as well get into the action.

Armed's foolhardy attack.

As he approaches the base, he spots a red team sentry. The opponent fires a Shotgun in his direction. Armed backs up and takes cover behind a rock. He knows that he is out of the effective range of the weapon. After a few seconds, the opponent ducks into the security of the base.

Seeing his chance to advance, Armed charges into the side entrance of the red base. As he goes in, he spots the red sentry running up to the top level of the base. Armed runs by the gate control panel and jumps down on the red flag. Of course, the red team is fully armed and waiting. Before Armed can take a step, he is cut down by a Rocket, a Battle Rifle burst, two SMGs, and a Frag Grenade.

Armed spawns again on the beach wall. He looks at the game time and shakes his head. He knows that the blue team will not get the cloth in this round.

Does this scenario sound familiar? I can guarantee that similar events are playing out hundreds of times every day over the Xbox *Live*™ network. Expert players learn from their mistakes. What mistakes were made during this ill-fated attack?

- The blue team had no plan.
- The blue team members hoarded weapons.
- Armed thought he knew the map. If he did, then he didn't use his knowledge effectively. When his teammate took the Sniper Rifle and Battle Rifle, he could have just jumped down and grabbed the second Battle Rifle.
- When the blue sniper didn't fire and Armed didn't hear any rocket fire, he should have anticipated that the other team had set up an ambush in the base.
- Armed didn't pay attention when his team indicators told him not to charge.
- Running into the side of the base meant that Armed was running right into an opponent with a Shotgun. He should have lobbed in a grenade or taken a different path. In fact, it was pure luck that he even made it past the red team guard.
- Armed should have opened the gate when he had the chance. This would have literally opened the door for a Warthog attack.
- Armed let his frustration get in the way of his logic. He should have armed himself with something better than a single SMG.
- Armed only communicated with his team when he wanted to yell at them.

These are all common mistakes in Halo® 2 game play. They are also examples of errors that are simple to correct. I see these sorts of blunders all the time on Xbox *Live*™. Not to mention all the times when I made mistakes that were just as costly.

During my time at Microsoft, I looked around for good Halo® strategy resources. This guide is my attempt to fill in the gaps that I found, which is why this book does not try to be all things to everyone.

This guide is not a level walk-through; it is not a one-time resource to help you finish the single player campaign. Instead, it is a resource to help gamers learn how to improve their performance in Halo 2 battles. You can then apply this knowledge in single player or multiplayer games. Essentially, this book will explore the strategy and tactics that will help you fulfill your potential as a Halo 2 player.

This book is based on the philosophy that there are various levels at which you can play Halo 2. For example, Chapter 2, Basic Combat, is designed to get you off to a fast start with the fundamentals of effective combat. When you are ready to build upon your basic combat skills by adding special tactics, you can read Chapter 5, Advanced Combat. In addition, you will benefit from practical advice from Halo 2 expert players. These tips and tricks will give you a decided advantage as you climb the Halo 2 levels much faster than you dreamed possible. With the help of this guide, you'll master combat and team strategy and expand your knowledge of weapons, and you will be able to embarrass your buddies at home or on Xbox *Live*™ in no time!

About Halo

Like many gamers, I was apprehensive about playing a console-based, first-person shooter (FPS). I simple didn't believe that I would enjoy the user interface. However, Halo 1 irreversibly altered my opinion. I wasn't the only one; Halo 1 was an enormous success. Not only is it the best selling game on the Xbox, but it also became a successful PC and Mac franchise when versions of the game were released for those platforms.

In addition to various platform versions, Halo 1 also has spawned novels—there are even rumors of some sort of a movie deal. This is all great news for Microsoft, but how does this help you as a gamer? The answer is quite simple; the more people who play Halo, the larger the Halo community. A larger community translates to more resources for you to use when you're looking to improve your game.

You should start by visiting Bungie.net, but don't stop there. Expand your search to other resources. The Unauthorized Halo Battle Guide website (www.halobattleguide.com) will point you to other useful sites such as http://halo.bungie.org, which is an excellent fan site. Refer to this site for all sorts of tips and tricks. Quite often, these fan sites will get a scoop on some sort of interesting way to use the Halo engine or manipulate the environment.

Some of these hacks require so much skill and effort that few people will take advantage of them. On the other hand, some of the tips are so useful that the majority of players adopt them. With online Halo 2 play, you can expect that there will be times when you wonder, "How did that guy do that?" When this happens, you can rush to one of these fan sites to search for the answer. Quite often, that answer will be waiting for you there.

You'll find that some Halo sites are purely for your entertainment. Probably the best example of a pure entertainment-focused Halo site is www.redvsblue.com. Others will go to great lengths to try to improve your fighting skills. Be sure to visit http://www.thegtc.com/videos.htm for Halo-related videos. These guys produced some cool Halo 1 material. Hopefully, they will continue the tradition with Halo 2.

Reading the Halo novels may not improve your game, but they will give you all sorts of background information about the Halo universe. If you're interested in enhancing your Halo experience by learning about the background mythology, then I recommend that you check them out.

Spoiler Alert!

Reading the next three paragraphs may give away information that you would rather get from the game or the Halo novels. Read them at your own risk!

At the end of *First Strike* by Eric Nylund, we find the Master Chief frantically trying to make his way back to Earth. Despite the best efforts of the human race, the Covenant have discovered the location of our home planet. Now it is up to the Master Chief to stop the Covenant from glassing Earth.

Although the motivation of the Covenant remains somewhat shrouded in mystery, we now know that the Covenant have been scouring galaxies in search of ancient artifacts. The Covenant believe that these artifacts hold the power to dominate the universe.

As with Halo 1, you can expect to be immediately immersed in the action. The enemy has new races to throw at you, new weapons to fire at you, and just as much hatred for the 'Flawless Cowboy.' The good news is that you also have a new bag of tricks. If you thought that the Grunts took off quickly when facing one barrel, imagine their surprise when you come at them with two!

Contents of this Battle Guide

This Battle Guide is designed to give you an edge by enabling you to learn about and master techniques and strategies organized by specific topics. This enables you to jump around and get the information you want when you want it. You can delve into this guide reading it cover to cover, or use it as a reference jumping to certain chapters for precise skills that you want to improve.

Warning:

Whatever you do, don't bypass Chapter 2, Basic Combat. It is the foundation upon which you will build all of your advanced skills. Even expert players can benefit from this primer.

Chapter 1: Introduction

You're about half-way through this chapter already—so I'm not going to ruin the ending for you.

Chapter 2: Basic Combat

This chapter is a quick introduction to the fundamentals of Halo 2 fights. Read this chapter first so that you can drop bad habits and avoid picking up new ones. As with many of the techniques covered in this book, these tactics will help you in any Halo 2 game, regardless of whether it's a multiplayer deathmatch or the single player campaign. After you have mastered these techniques, you can have more fun with the advanced topics.

Chapter 3: Weapons

The Weapons chapter provides detailed information about your entire arsenal. After reading this chapter, you will have a complete understanding of the strengths and weaknesses of each weapon. Use this information to become a fearsome force no matter what you have in your hands.

Chapter 4: Vehicles

There have been some changes to the Halo 1 vehicles and some new ones added to the game. Read this chapter to learn all about the changes and the features of the new vehicles in Halo 2. In addition, you'll learn vehicle-specific strategies.

Chapter 5: Advanced Combat

Building on the information in Chapter 2, Basic Combat, this chapter explores fighting tactics that are used by the Halo 2 experts. After reading this chapter, you will have the information you need to become an expert Halo 2 gamer in your own right.

Chapter 6: Solo Strategy

The strategy section is an in-depth analysis of popular Halo 2 single player maneuvers. You will be able to use this information in any game type. You can also use these tips to help you get through the single player campaign.

Chapter 7: Team Strategy

Strategy gains a factor of complexity when you are playing as part of a team. In this chapter, you will read about offensive and defensive team strategies. Use this information to help your team win games such as Capture the Flag and Assault. Since you will be able to coordinate a squad, this chapter emphasizes real-world military strategy.

Chapter 8: Multiplayer Maps

Knowing the terrain is a fundamental requirement of performing well in a Halo 2 game. This chapter gives you the knowledge that you should have before you even step foot on a Halo 2 map. Information such as weapon location, defensive strategies, and offensive strategies are included for each 'out of the box' multiplayer map.

Chapter 9: Level Ranking System

Halo 2 features online matchmaking against players of similar skill levels. Learn how this system determines the outcome of each game and what you can do to quickly increase your personal level.

Chapter 10: Wort Wort Wort! Halo 2 Etiquette

Halo 2 etiquette is an understanding between players of what is and isn't acceptable—not the rules of play. Just as there are cultural differences in etiquette in the real world, there are different interpretations of game etiquette among players—on your own team or around the world on Xbox Live©. This chapter examines a number of controversial etiquette issues. It is my hope that this material will act as a catalyst for preemptive discussions among Halo 2 players of acceptable behaviors to ensure everyone enjoys playing nicely together.

Appendix A: Halo 2 Glossary

The Glossary contains a reference of common terminology used by Halo 2 gamers. You've got to talk the talk before you can walk the walk.

Crew 116

www.crew116.com

After playing Halo 2 for a while, it was obvious to me that I needed some lessons in Halo 2 multiplayer gaming. It was also obvious whom I should contact. This group is known as "Crew 116" and they have been playing multiplayer Halo at least once a week since Halo 1 was released.

Crew 116:

You may think that the Crew 116 moniker has something to do with the Master Chief's designation as John 117; however, this is not the case. The group became known as Crew 116 because they used to play in building 116 on the Microsoft campus—long before *The Fall of Reach* was written.

There has been speculation that someone at Bungie may have influenced author Eric Nylund's decision to name the Master Chief 'John 117'. However, there has been no confirmation of this rumor.

In exchange for a bribe of pizza, I went to one of the Crew 116 Halo nights and played with some of the best. They are certainly the best team at Microsoft so I invited them to contribute to this guide and they honored me with their wealth of knowledge. Throughout this book, you will find useful tips and tricks from Crew 116. Here is an introduction to some of the team members:

Crew 116 Profiles

Gamertag: char

Favorite Halo 2 Weapon: Battle Rifle, Sword

Favorite Halo 2 Multiplayer Level: Midship, Burial Mounds

Playing Style: I play mid-map suppression. You'll often find me roaming the midfield playing defense; my goal is to keep the enemy away from our base and help support an offensive push.

Covering the field.

Greatest Strength: There are a lot of attributes that make someone a good player. In team games, however, I'd say that field awareness is probably the most important. If you don't understand what's going on, you can't play effectively. It's critical that you know where your teammates and the opponents are. Which direction are the opponents pushing, and can you help defend against that? Is your team being flanked? Does your team have control over important areas of the map? Knowing these things will help you support your team well and be more effective in a team game.

Every Expert Halo Gamer Should: Start with Basic Free For All (FFA) skills. Learn the weapons inside and out, which weapons trump others, how to grenade, when to dual wield (DW), and so forth. Once you have that down, start working on team play tactics.

Halo Game Play Philosophy: Have fun! The Alpha and Beta really built up certain expectations about some players. I didn't always have a good time having to play seriously and be concerned with rank, win percentage, and so forth. Sometimes you want to take it seriously and kick ass, and sometimes you want to take it easy and have a few fun games with your friends. The Alpha/Beta weren't really conducive to that, and it reminded me why I play the game in the first place; it's fun to play with your friends.

Gamertag: Striker

Favorite Halo 2 Weapon: Battle Rifle

Favorite Halo 2 Multiplayer Level: Ivory Tower

Playing Style: Deny access to any resource capable of giving the edge to my opponent. When I'm healthy, I force battles quickly before my opponents can prepare themselves. When I'm weak, I avoid battle while I seek out health, weapons, and ammo.

Keep an eye on the big guns.

Greatest Strength: Understanding the limits of the game, and pushing the envelope as far as what can be accomplished.

Every Expert Halo Gamer Should: Be proficient with all the weapons and understand what makes each of them unique (for example, knowing when the Battle Rifle beats the Shotgun).

Also, have grenade skills to complement your playing style. Make sure you have the necessary throws for any game type you want to excel at (for example, platform to platform on the Halo 1 Wizard level).

Be able to communicate effectively with your team. Your team should have a vocabulary that uniquely identifies any location or scenario of importance (such as "sniper in pistol cave").

Halo Game Play Philosophy: Find and abuse any dominant strategy for a given game type. There is no such thing as a cheap or lame tactic or strategy. If you've got something that's working for you, use it and abuse it.

Gamertag: tantrum

Favorite Halo 2 Weapon: Battle Rifle, Covenant Beam Rifle

Favorite Halo 2 Multiplayer Level: Ivory Tower

Playing Style: It depends on the game type. For FFA Slayer, I try to set up in an advantageous area and own from there. For Team Slayer, I try to stay out of harm's way, get good weapons, and stay with my team. For CTF team games, I tend to throw myself at the problem, regardless of dying. I feel this can be very helpful to the team at times.

Greatest Strength: Thinking.

Every Expert Halo Gamer Should: Know the maps inside out. Also, remember what weapons you have and what their reload state is, and use the appropriate ones for the situation—including grenades. Gather as much information as possible at all times about where things are happening—this means "screen cheating" a lot of the time, either off your team or enemy. Have good aim and go for headshots with the appropriate weapons. Communicate well with your team in team games.

Halo Game Play Philosophy: Strategy will often defeat skill.

> ### Note:
> *Screen cheating* is the practice of looking at other players' screens during a game. Some people consider this cheating because you can see where the other players are located by what you see on their screen. See Chapter 10 for more on screen cheating.

Gamertag: DJ 116

Favorite Halo 2 Weapon: Battle Rifle

Favorite Halo 2 Multiplayer Level: Midship

Playing Style: I am a team leader. My team will push for lockdown and then unleash a full coordinated push at the base. I usually snipe until we gain control of the map and then push in with my team to control the enemy base. Often we can link multiple captures in a row.

Greatest Strength: Leadership

Every Expert Halo Gamer Should: Communicate any 10 square foot spot on the map in two syllables or less.

Halo Game Play Philosophy: There is no 'I' in team.

Gamertag: MrJukes

Note:

Although MrJukes is not an actual member of Crew 116, his tips have been included because he distinguished himself while playing with the guys in Crew 116.

Favorite Halo 2 Weapon: Battle Rifle

Favorite Halo 2 Multiplayer Level: Ivory Tower

Playing Style: I'm a utility player. I'm good at surveying the battlefield and knowing what has to be done. I can plug the gap wherever it is needed. I am also usually pretty good at not getting killed. My kill-to-death ratio is generally fairly high.

Greatest Strength: Patience. Some call it camping; I call it strategy. I play the game to accomplish the objective. If my objective is to prevent you from taking the flag, I'm not going to be running all over the map. I stay close to my objective.

Every Expert Halo Gamer Should: Not be afraid to use Grenades. It's much easier to kill people without shields. I try not to stockpile grenades. If I'm not sure if there is somebody waiting around a corner, I'll just chuck a grenade in front of me just in case.

I also spend a lot of time running routes that most people cannot take or that most people do not expect you to take. If there is somebody waiting for you to run up a ramp, I'd rather take the alternative route, like make the difficult jump up the side, and surprise them.

Halo Game Play Philosophy: It's much easier to shoot people in the back.

Getting the drop on someone.

Chapter 2: Basic Combat

This chapter is an introduction to Halo 2 combat. Although these tactics and strategies may seem obvious to experienced players, it's absolutely essential to have a solid grounding in the basics before moving on to advanced strategy. Furthermore, these basic combat strategies will help you in the single player campaign as well as multi-player games.

Because a number of these subjects are covered in detail in later chapters, this chapter is meant to be a quick read. If you want to become an expert Halo 2 gamer, you must have a solid grasp of basic combat. Make sure you have fully mastered these basics before you attempt to expand your arsenal with more advanced tactics and strategies.

Run and Gun

The first rule of playing Halo 2 is that you cannot stand still. You have to move around or you will be a sitting duck. Take this advice to heart: learn to be a crack shot while running at full speed.

Keep moving or you will watch more than you play.

Practice Tip:

You should practice running around and firing at specific targets. For example, you should be able to explode a Covenant fusion core with a single Battle Rifle burst—even while you are running and jumping.

Cyclic Fights (a.k.a. 'Circle Strafe')

When players try to protect their backs, they often end up with battles that go around in circles. No one wants to turn around, so players will usually *strafe*, or run, sideways. Get used to this style of fighting; you will need to learn how to run and gun in a tight circle.

Crew 116 Advice: Cyclic Fighting

One very basic problem that beginners have is that they don't keep their thumbs on the d-pads. If they want to look left, they will push the d-pad all the way left and then release (physically taking their finger off the pad). Expert players will keep their fingers locked on the analog pad—except for the short periods when they are reloading/meleeing/picking up weapons/switching weapons/jumping. In addition, expert players get comfortable slowly adjusting their view by pressing the analog pad less than 100% in one direction.

—DJ 116

Practice Tip:

To practice fighting in a circle, walk around another player while keeping your reticle on his or her head. Learn to do this without taking your thumbs off the analog pads. Once you get the hang of it, try doing the same thing while your target moves erratically.

Crew 116 Advice: Aiming

My old calculation for the Halo 1 pistol was this: Let's say you hit 100% of your shots when aiming for the body, but only 50% when aiming for the head. If you always aim for the body, it takes about five hits to kill. If you aim only for the head, it takes three hits; but you don't hit every shot, so it actually takes you six headshots. Remember that the last few shots will be more effective if you have already weakened the target's shields. If you switch from body to head after hitting two body shots, you will generally average about four shots. This is the preferred method.

—Striker

Aim Smart

Many players commonly believe that headshots are always better than body shots. However, this is a myth. Shooting at the head doesn't make any difference until the opponent's shield is down. The obvious exceptions to this rule are the Sniper Rifles. One headshot with the Sniper weapon can take out any player—regardless of his shield status.

Therefore, the best strategy is to aim high once your opponent's shields are down. After the shield is down, a single headshot from a number of weapons can finish off a player. When you hit a player's shield, you will see the shield flare. If you don't see this happening, it is best to go for the winning headshot.

Certain weapons are coded such that they cause extra headshot damage to an unshielded player. Some of the weapons that feature this headshot bonus are the Sniper Rifle, the Beam Rifle, the Battle Rifle, and the Magnum.

Reloading

One of the ways to balance a weapon is to slow the time that it takes for the weapon to reload. This means that the more powerful weapons will take longer to reload. Don't get caught in the middle of a battle with nothing in your clip. Make sure that you reload whenever it is safe to do so. Even if you have only taken a few shots, reload if you know that you have the time.

If you are dual wielding, you might want to consider staggering your fire. By not starting your fire with both weapons simultaneously, you will have some ammo left in one when the other is reloading.

If you find yourself reloading both your weapons, remember that you still have the option to melee or chuck a grenade.

Your Arsenal

You can only carry two weapons with you at a time. Unless you have a specific plan that requires special weapons, you should always carry a short-range and a long-range weapon. This keeps your options open and allows for a lot of flexibility in your fighting style.

Dual Wielding

Dual wielding (DW) is definitely one of the coolest features that came with the release of Halo 2. However, firing two guns comes with some disadvantages. When your hands are full, you cannot use grenades. In addition, when you are reloading both guns, the actions are serialized so it takes longer than a single weapon. Nonetheless, DW can be very effective at short range. You should try DW and decide if it works for you.

Winning Tactic:

Remember that a quick melee will drop one of your guns and give you back your grenades.

Shields

Do not fight when your shields are down. Bug out and live to fight another battle. If you take cover, you can give your shields a chance to recharge. On the other hand, if you try to fight, many weapons will finish you with a single head shot.

In later chapters, we will examine occasions when you might choose to stay in the battle. However, for now, just focus on fighting with those shields up.

> "better to retire...than push a bad position"
> —Viper, *Top Gun*

Shields lighting up.

Motion Detector— Watch Your Back!

You must always remember that your back is incredibly vulnerable. Even when you are retreating, it is best to face your enemy. Unless you are going for maximum speed, you should retreat backward.

The best way to protect your back is to use your motion detector. Not all game types use the motion detector but when it's there, you must use it. If you do not, other players will sneak up behind you and smite you with a single melee attack to the back of the head.

Evasion

Don't underestimate the value of making your opponent miss. While it is true that you should first focus on hitting your target, some fights will be decided by a good dodge. The basic evasion tactic is *strafing*. You should use a back and forth sidestepping movement as your standard evasion technique. Some people like to move laterally quickly; this is the *short strafe*. Others prefer to move further to one side and then go back; this is known as the *long strafe*.

Some players like to jump or crouch. However, Crew 116 strongly recommends that you stick with strafing moves. I think that Striker put it best when he told me that, "jumping makes your trajectory predictable. Your goal is to be unpredictable." This may sound strange to those of you who are big fans of the evasive jump, but the fact remains that the best players do not jump unless they are getting away from an explosion.

You won't see many players crouching during a battle. This is because sidestepping and jumping are easier to learn and they allow you to keep moving. Once you are effectively strafing during battles, then you can experiment with crouching or jumping to see if they work for you. Because most players will aim for the headshot bonus, these techniques can be effective at times.

Shadows and Cover

Perhaps the most obvious technique to stay in the game is to use cover and dark areas. If you are trying to get in close, you should stay out of sight. Do not run out into the open.

A well-hidden elite.

> ### Winning Tactic:
> The area in front of each Waterworks base is an open killing zone. Unless you have a specific objective in mind, don't run into this area.

The Better Part of Valor

You cannot win every battle so do not try. You must choose when to engage and when to evade. As stated previously, a good time to back down is when your shields are down. However, there are many other examples of being at a clear disadvantage such as being badly outgunned or facing superior numbers.

Of course, this isn't a black and white rule; much of this book is fundamentally about the strategy of when to engage. Don't expect to make the right decision every time. If you lose, you should ask yourself if you should have avoided the battle.

A SPARTAN deciding whether he should engage.

"The rules for making war are:

If you outnumber enemy forces ten to one, surround them.

If you outnumber them five to one, attack them.

If you outnumber them two to one, divide them.

If you are equal, find an advantageous battle.

If you are fewer, defend against them.

If you are much weaker, evade them."

—Sun Tzu, *The Art of War*

Weapon Selection

To be an effective Halo 2 gamer, there are two rules about weapons that you must respect at all times:

1. **Hit what you shoot at.**
2. **Use the right weapon at the right time.**

The first rule is so obvious that it requires no explanation; however, the second rule requires clarification. Some players will choose a favorite weapon and pretty much use that weapon whenever they have it in their arsenal. While it is important to be familiar with the Halo 2 weapons, make sure that your comfort with one weapon doesn't become a disadvantage. Use the right tool for the right job.

As a player, you should be well versed in the following basic offensive and defensive guidelines for the Halo 2 weapons. See Chapter 3, Weapons, for more details about weapons and their usage tactics.

Use the right weapon for the right job.

When You Have It...

Human Weapons

Magnum Pistol. The Magnum is not as powerful as the Halo 1 Pistol, but most people believe that this is a positive change. The Halo 2 version has some nice features; it can be dual wielded and it has a lightning fast rate of fire. Use it for headshots when your opponent's shields are down—even at range you will find it effective. However, don't even dream of using it against shields—all you will do is give away your position.

Submachine Gun (SMG). This is one of the easiest weapons to find in Halo 2. Because of this fact, you'll end up using it a fair bit. One SMG is not a great threat so try to dual wield them or combine one with precise grenade throws. Dual SMGs are great for short-range fights and for spraying an opponent who attempts to close on your position.

Shotgun. The Shotgun is a powerful weapon. In fact, it's one of the few weapons in the game that can get you a one shot victory. On small maps, you should generally strive to have either the Shotgun or the Plasma Sword with you at all times. They are the best weapons in a face-to-face conflict.

When you have the shottie, try to get in close and bring opponents down quickly. Don't use this weapon at range. Even at medium range, the Halo 2 Shotgun is ineffective. Have another weapon ready for distant opponents.

Battle Rifle. This is a great range weapon. It features semi-auto burst fire and a 2X scope. Some people will use the burst mode for tight combat, but it isn't the weapon of choice when you are in close. Keep your distance and cut people down as they try to advance on your position. If you catch someone in the open, you should have an easy frag with this weapon. On medium to large maps, try to have this rifle available.

The new Battle Rifle.

Sniper Rifle. This is the ultimate range weapon. One headshot and your foe will hit the mat. Just remember that you are firing rounds with contrails—after a couple of shots, move to another spot. It is difficult to aim this weapon in a close fight so few people try.

A SPARTAN using the Sniper Rifle on Waterworks.

Rocket Launcher. The Rocket Launcher is the most powerful hand-held weapon in the game. However, don't convince yourself that it's the right choice for all occasions. The launcher has the largest splash area of any weapon. If your opponent is too close, you will likely end up tagging yourself when you fire. You should use this weapon to win medium- and long-range battles.

When it comes to vehicles, there is no question that this is the weapon of choice. Use the new tracking feature to take out any vehicles in your path.

Reloading powerful weapons takes time.

Winning Tactic:

When firing the Rocket Launcher, aim at your target's feet. This will minimize your chance of missing and maximize the splash damage. I saw a newbie take out two Hunters with one shot because she aimed at their feet.

Fragmentation Grenades. Use Fragmentation Grenades when you don't have a clear line of sight to your target. They will bounce off pretty much everything in the Halo environment, so you can throw them around corners with ease.

Covenant Weapons

Plasma Pistol. This was not a popular Halo 1 weapon, but it can be used strategically in Halo 2. Dual wield this weapon with some other gun and take advantage of the plasma burst option. The burst will take out an enemy's shield and the other weapon can finish him.

Plasma Rifle. The Plasma Rifle in Halo 2 does not pack the plasma stun effect of the Halo 1 version. This means that you can't freeze your foe like in the good ol' days. This gun is still useful though, especially when you DW two of them.

Plasma Sword. Along with the Shotgun, the Plasma Sword is one of the top two short-range weapons in the game. The lunge feature of the sword is just brutal; it's one of the most deadly moves in the game. Wait for the reticle to turn red and then pull the trigger. It's a very rewarding one hit take down.

Needler. The tracking ability of the needles is most useful when your opponent is in the open. The best plan is to fire into an open space from a covered position. Jump out, light someone up, and then run behind your cover. Don't expect it to drop people quickly, but dual wielding this weapon can be a lot of fun.

A SPARTAN with the Covenant Needler.

Covenant Carbine. This is the Covenant's answer to the Battle Rifle. However, the Carbine fires single shots. It is a great range weapon but difficult to use in close combat.

Two elites patrolling with the Covenant carbine.

Beam Rifle. This weapon is the Covenant's sniper gun so you should use it as you would the human Sniper Rifle.

Brute Shot. The Brute Shot is a fun weapon and it is excellent for medium-range battles. It is powerful, but it takes some getting used to. The rounds bounce, so you can even use the Brute Shot around corners. This makes it a great all around weapon; just don't expect it to take out people as fast as the Rocket Launcher.

Plasma Grenades. Plasma Grenades are often called 'sticky' grenades because you can get them to stick to some surfaces. If I have any of these, I usually switch to them so that I can quickly stick an opponent who gets the drop on me.

A plasma grenade exploding.

When They Have It...

Human Weapons

Magnum Pistol. If someone comes at you with a single Magnum, either he has made a mistake or he is trying to reel you in. Take the opportunity to engage, but your safest play is to retreat and spray the advancing player. If he continues to advance, you will win the battle; however, if he stops, then he was trying a feint. He has a strong short-range weapon in his pocket and he was trying to get you to attack. In the latter case, use a range weapon to take him down.

Submachine Gun (SMG). A single SMG is not a huge threat but dual SMGs are lethal. This is a spray weapon so expect your attacker to keep a little distance. If you have a powerful short-range weapon, you may be tempted to charge. However, don't try to close ground against two SMGs unless you're already pretty close and you're healthy.

Shotgun. In contrast to the single Magnum attack, if someone comes at you with the Shotgun, you had better get away fast or stop him even faster. If you have some space, spray weapons (the SMG and Plasma Rifle) and range weapons (the Sniper Rifle, Battle Rifle, and Covenant Beam Rifle) work well against a Shotgun.

Battle Rifle. When facing the Battle Rifle, your best course of action is to avoid the attacker's line of fire while you get close to his position. Another option is to pull out a Sniper Rifle. The Battle Rifle is a great range weapon, but it won't take out someone as fast as a Sniper Rifle.

A Battle Rifle showdown.

Sniper Rifle. Remember that it only takes one shot to get shut down by this gun. As with other range weapons, you should immediately use cover and evasion. If you have a good range weapon (for example, the Battle Rifle or a Covenant Carbine), you can prevent the sniper from keeping his zoom by hitting him every now and then. The best ways to take out a sniper are to get close to him, counterattack with a long-range weapon, or flood his position with grenades.

Rocket Launcher. If you are close enough to your foe, he may fear a suicide and decide not to use this weapon. If you aren't right in his face, you'll have to take cover. Just remember that taking cover from a rocket isn't like taking cover from any other weapon. You not only need to be behind something, you also need to get far enough away from the explosion. In other words, don't just hide behind a corner. Run around the corner and keep going.

Note that good players will aim for your feet, which is why jumping away from a rocket is one of the few occasions where jumping is recommended.

Fragmentation Grenades. You must run away from grenades. You may choose to run forward if you think that it will get you farther away from the explosion. See Chapter 5, Advanced Combat, for advanced grenade tactics.

Covenant Weapons

Plasma Pistol. Remember that a single overloaded burst from this pistol can drop your shield. If the attacker misses with a burst shot, then the same guidelines as the Magnum apply. On the other hand, if your shield is knocked out, you will have to drop the attacker fast or get away so that you can recharge your shield.

Plasma Rifle. Without the Halo 1 stun effect, this is a weaker weapon. However, an attacker can now dual wield this gun. Use your strafing dodge to avoid getting hit and either return fire or take cover. The decision will depend on what you are carrying.

Needler. If you are able to take some sort of cover, you will fair well in a fight against the Needler. Remember that the needles have limited tracking ability. If you are in the open, you had better take cover or silence your adversary quickly. Even after he is down, the needles already fired could finish you.

Plasma Sword. Get away! You will have very little time to react if someone gets near you with this knife. The best thing to do is retreat backward as you spray the attacker. Ideally, use dual SMG fire or a good medium-range weapon. If you have the Shotgun, you can try to get the first shot in, but don't think that you'll get a second chance. Even if the attacker misses with the first lunge, he may still be able to get you quickly.

The deadly Plasma Sword.

Covenant Carbine. If you have a good short-range weapon, get close to the opponent and fight up close and personal. If you have a strong medium- to long-range weapon, you can have a showdown.

A close look at the Covenant Carbine.

Beam Rifle. Treat this weapon as you would the human Sniper Rifle. One shot can put you out of action.

Brute Shot. It is tough to fight against the Brute Shot. Even if you take cover, your opponent can bounce the rounds toward you. Your saving grace may be the fact that this weapon generally doesn't finish you with one hit. If you have a powerful short-range weapon, you may want to make a feint, retreat, and go for a short-range ambush.

Plasma Grenades. Sticking someone with a Plasma Grenade is fun, but it sucks when you see plasma burning all over your own screen. The basic principle is the same as for Frag Grenades—get far away from the explosion. However, you also have to do everything you can to prevent a Plasma Grenade from touching you. If you see a high one coming at you, sidestep and advance to get away from the explosion. If you think that one is going to land in front of you, dodge it and retreat.

> **Winning Tactic:**
> If you get stuck with a Plasma Grenade, run right up to an opponent. The explosion hopefully will take the other player with you so you can force a tie.

A good time to dodge.

> **Winning Tactic:**
> Take some time to get used to all the weapons in the game. You will find it frustrating when you're losing with a weapon that you don't like, but eventually it will pay off. You should be deadly with any weapon in your hand—or in both your hands.

Chapter 3: Weapons

Designing weapons may seem like an easy task, but it is actually a delicate balancing act. If the game designers create a weapon that is too powerful, then players will fight to get to the spawn spots for that weapon. Once a player has that all-powerful weapon, she would be able to dominate. On the other hand, if the game designers create a gun that is too weak, then no one will use the weapon and all the development, testing, and animation cycles for that weapon becomes wasted work.

The Halo 1 weapons were well done, but they also showed how a few mistakes can greatly impact the game. For example, the Halo 1 Human Pistol was clearly overpowered and the Needler was commonly considered underpowered. I would argue that the Needler was a strategic weapon, but I can't defend the Pistol at all.

The Pistol was meant to be a backup option—remember that it was the first weapon that the Master Chief was given in Halo 1. Instead of being a last resort, it became the weapon of choice in Halo 1 tournaments. Expert players would actually turn down their look sensitivity so they could improve their accuracy with the Pistol. Many people also argued that it was illogical to have a scope on the Pistol when even weapons such as the Assault Rifle didn't have one. By the way, you can rest assured that the Halo 2 Magnum Pistol is not as powerful as the Halo 1 Human Pistol.

This chapter examines the vital statistics for the Halo 2 weaponry. You will be more effective in all situations when you are armed with an understanding of each weapon.

> "Expert players must be proficient with all the weapons and understand what makes them each unique."
> —Striker, Crew 116

Weapon Descriptions

Human Weapons

M6C Magnum Pistol

Dual Wield: Yes

Clip Size: 12

Ammo Limit: 48

Rate of Fire: Semi-automatic

Effective Range: Short

Reload Time: Very slow

Features: John Woo-style action and a headshot bonus

Strengths: The ability to dual-wield this gun and its rapid fire rate combine for an effective punch against bodies. This also is one of the weapons that boasts a headshot bonus so use it when your target's shields are down.

Weaknesses: Not useful against shields.

Details: Don't waste your ammo firing at a shielded target. Although it's only a semi-automatic weapon, dual wielding Magnums has proven to be effective in some cases. For example, you can use this technique when playing the 'Snipers' game type. Simply sneak up on snipers and use two Magnums for a point blank cut down. Although this weapon is slow to load, another good example is games without shields. Use dual Magnums and aim high.

The Magnum Pistol.

Sub Machine Gun (SMG)

Dual Wield: Yes

Clip Size: 60

Ammo Limit: 180

Rate of Fire: Fast

Effective Range: Medium

Reload Time: Medium

Features: None

Strengths: The large clip makes this is an effective spray weapon. Dual wield two SMGs to cut up players at medium range.

Weaknesses: Limited range and causes little damage by itself, especially against shields.

Details: The SMG is often the weapon that you're carrying when you spawn. One SMG doesn't pack a tremendous punch but two of them are a great medium range combination. If an attacker confronts you with the Shotgun, Magnum, or the Plasma Sword, retreat and spray the aggressor as he advances. If you are out of his effective range, you will have the advantage.

When facing an adversary with a good range weapon, be careful. Don't be tempted into running out into the open against a Battle Rifle or Covenant Carbine. The SMG will not win anything other than a close range battle against a rifle. However, most automatic weapons in Halo 2 are very accurate for the first few shots. When you're in close, just hold down the trigger, but at range you'll increase your accuracy with short, controlled bursts.

The new Sub Machine Gun.

M90 Shotgun

Dual Wield: No

Clip Size: 12

Ammo Limit: 36

Rate of Fire: Slow

Effective Range: Short

Reload Time: Slow

Features: None

Strengths: At close range, this weapon is deadly. If you are close enough, even a fully shielded opponent will go down with one shot.

Weaknesses: This gun doesn't work well past short range and it is slow to reload.

Details: If you're on a small map or working in a building, you may choose to use the shottie. At short range, most people will choose the Plasma Sword or the Shotgun, which are both devastating when you're in close. Quite often, your own personal preference determines which one is better for you. However, the Shotgun has the advantage of letting you stay put as you fire at close targets. For example, you may be guarding a spot that allows you to fire from above. You would have to jump down if you attacked with the Plasma Sword, but you could stay on your perch if you use the Shotgun. On a map like Lockout the sword lunge may even cause you to jump off the edge. The Plasma Sword is discussed later in this chapter.

It's probably fair to say that most people make the mistake of forgetting the limitations of this gun. It is deadly, but obviously it doesn't make you invincible. If you're faced with multiple targets, keep in mind that you may be able to get the first one easily, but you will then need to get close to the others. If your opponents are smart, they will back up and spray you while you try to close the gap. Don't charge into their spray. Instead switch to a medium range weapon or find a safe way to flank the enemy. This isn't Doom© where the Shotgun is the preferred gun for long range accuracy.

The Shotgun loads slowly, so don't run out of ammo as you enter a fight. This generally is not a problem unless you're playing the 'Shotguns' game type. (And even then, most players won't survive long enough to use all of the ammo.) The Shotguns game type can be a blast. Try to use cover and short strafe dodges to force the other players to miss their first shot. One miss against a Shotgun is all it takes to give you the advantage.

The Halo 2 Shotgun.

BR55 Battle Rifle

Dual Wield: No

Clip Size: 36

Ammo Limit: 108

Rate of Fire: Fast (3-shot bursts)

Effective Range: Long

Reload Time: Medium

Features: Scope (2X) Three round burst fire.

Strengths: Extremely versatile weapon. Headshot bonus.

Weaknesses: Close range battles require excellent accuracy.

Details: This is my favorite weapon. I recommend it as your medium range weapon of choice, and the burst mode is a decent option at short range. However, I certainly wouldn't recommend using this as your primary short range weapon. You'll have to decide whether it works for you.

The Battle Rifle's flexibility is its greatest asset. It's one of the most versatile of the Halo 2 weapons. Just don't ask me how a SPARTAN can use a scope while wearing his helmet.

If you're playing the Midship level, you can use the Battle Rifle to irritate the opposite base. Using the Battle Rifle scope, you can easily distract the other team from your attacking force—you'll probably even poach a few kills. Having this weapon is a great advantage in open space. Zanzibar and Waterworks both include great examples of Battle Rifle-friendly terrain.

The Battle Rifle.

S2 AM Sniper Rifle

Dual Wield: No

Clip Size: 4

Ammo Limit: 20

Rate of Fire: Medium

Effective Range: Long

Reload Time: Slow

Features: Dual setting scope (5X and 10X), night scope.

Strengths: Significant damage including a headshot bonus, and a powerful scope. It's one of the weapons that can finish a fully shielded adversary with a single shot.

Weaknesses: Slow to reload and it's tough to aim at close range.

Details: The Human Sniper Rifle is a very popular weapon—probably because many people enjoy the visceral satisfaction associated with sniping. In Halo 2, it's the most efficient means of getting a one shot frag from long range.

The main change with the Halo 2 Sniper Rifle is the obvious recoil of the gun. Unlike in Halo 1, you may have to adjust your aim between shots.

Just like any other weapon, the Sniper Rifle comes with its drawbacks. For starters, the clip is small and the reload time is long. However, the most glaring disadvantage of the Sniper Rifle is the fact that its round leaves contrails, so you might as well be firing tracer rounds. No other weapon reveals your position in such a pronounced fashion. When you first try the Sniper Rifle, you may not think that the contrail is a big disadvantage, but as soon as you play against some skilled opponents, it will become painfully clear that trails are like a red cape to a bull. After you fire a couple of rounds, you should seriously consider moving to another spot. Unless you are playing a team game and you're confident in your team's ability to protect you, you should combine the Sniper Rifle with a weapon suited for close combat.

See Chapter 5, Advanced Combat, for more on the Sniper Rifle.

M19 SSM Rocket Launcher

Dual Wield: No

Clip Size: 2

Ammo Limit: 6

Rate of Fire: Slow

Effective Range: Long

Reload Time: Very Slow

Features: Scope (2X), vehicle lock for rocket tracking.

Strengths: Most damaging handheld weapon in the game and it boasts significant splash damage.

Weaknesses: Small clip and slow reload.

Details: When it comes to attacking vehicles, the Rocket Launcher is the weapon of choice. Zoom in on a vehicle and hold your trigger to get a lock. After a couple of seconds, the reticle will turn red to show that you're locked on. When you fire a locked rocket, it will follow the target vehicle. It is possible for the vehicle to dodge—especially if there is something between the incoming shell and the vehicle—but the targeting is generally effective.

The Rocket Launcher boasts the greatest splash damage of any handheld weapon. Make sure you aim accordingly to make the most of this feature. As mentioned in Chapter 2, Basic Combat, the most effective way to maximize the splash damage is to fire at an opponent's feet. A shot aimed at the body might sail right past the target. You can achieve the same effect if you're able to hit anything that is nearby—try a wall

The Human Sniper Rifle.

The new Rocket Launcher.

behind the player or even another opponent. The splash damage of this weapon is not as damaging as the Halo 1 version. For example, you probably won't be able to shoot players on a ledge by aiming at them from below.

M9 HE-DP Fragmentation Grenades

Dual Wield: N/A

Clip Size: N/A

Ammo Limit: 4

Rate of Fire: Medium

Effective Range: Long

Reload Time: N/A

Features: None

Strengths: Ability to bounce these pineapples. They cause splash damage.

Weaknesses: You can only carry four.

Details: The Fragmentation Grenade has a short fuse that activates the first time the grenade hits the ground. Keep in mind that the fuse might activate before actually touching the ground if you happen to hit a level portion of a rough surface. Human Grenades are not as effective against shields as Plasma Grenades, but they can cause a great deal of damage. Based on this fact, you should save your Frag Grenades for use against unshielded bodies. Read Chapter 5, Advanced Combat, for more about effective grenade tactics. As with rockets, the Fragmentation Grenade is not as powerful as the Halo 1 version. You should try out the new grenades to get used to the new splash radius.

A Fragmentation Grenade.

Stationary Turret

Dual Wield: N/A

Clip Size: N/A

Ammo Limit: Infinite

Rate of Fire: Fast

Effective Range: Medium

Reload Time: N/A

Features: None

Strengths: Infinite ammo with some spray.

Weaknesses: The gun is, by definition, stationary, and there is no cover while you are firing this destructible weapon.

Details: Everyone enjoyed cutting down aliens with the Covenant Shade Turret in Halo 1. Now you can enjoy stationary guns in multiplayer modes as well. Unlike the Shade, this turret is destructible. However, it is fully automatic, works at decent range, and it has infinite ammunition.

There will be times during multiplayer games when this gun will be useful. For example, the turrets on top of the red Zanzibar base can cut down attackers who attempt to flee with the flag. Just remember that you have no cover when you are using this weapon. As most of us did on *The Truth and Reconciliation* Halo 1 level, snipers love to check stationary guns for easy prey.

The Human Stationary Turret.

Covenant Weapons

Plasma Pistol

Dual Wield: Yes

Clip Size: 100

Ammo Limit: N/A

Rate of Fire: As fast as you can pull the trigger.

Effective Range: Medium

Reload Time: N/A

Features: Overload burst with limited tracking.

Strengths: Overcharged burst ball will drop shields.

Weaknesses: Single shots are ineffective.

Details: A generally underrated weapon in Halo 1. Not only did it have a burst that would take out shields, but the speed that you could pull your trigger determined its rate of fire. I didn't make use of this weapon the first time I went through the single player campaign. However, if I were to do it again, I would use this gun extensively. Against Elites, you simply hit them with a locked on burst and then switch to the Human Pistol for a quick take down.

In Halo 2, the Plasma Pistol is still not a very fearsome weapon on its own, but with dual wielding it is far more interesting. You can use the Plasma Pistol to quickly take down a foe's shields and then quickly finish him with the weapon in your other hand.

> ### Crew 116 Advice: DW Combination
>
> DW with a Plasma Pistol and Magnum can be a very quick kill. Hit 'em with a ball and headshot them.
>
> —*char*

Plasma Rifle

Dual Wield: Yes

Clip Size: 100

Ammo Limit: N/A

Rate of Fire: Fast

Effective Range: Medium

Reload Time: N/A

Features: None

Strengths: Automatic fire that works well against shields.

Weaknesses: The Halo 1 stun effect is gone. As with other plasma weapons, this rifle overheats.

Details: At first, the Halo 2 Plasma Rifle doesn't seem as powerful as the Halo 1 version. I'm sure that many Halo fans will miss the stun effect that came with the old Plasma Rifle. However, you can now hold two of these and they fire faster. These changes will probably ease the fans' pain. This is a dramatic gun to dual wield because it lights your screen up with plasma.

This is a good medium range weapon. If you only have one, you might want to use it against shields and then chuck a grenade to finish off your prey. As with the SMG, you generally want to DW this rifle with another weapon. Do not let this weapon overheat. An overheated plasma weapon cannot fire at all. It is a much better strategy to fire until you're getting close to overheating and then wait for the weapon to cool. This gives you the option to overheat the weapon in an emergency.

The Plasma Pistol.

The Plasma Rifle.

Brute Plasma Rifle

Dual Wield: Yes

Clip Size: 100

Ammo Limit: N/A

Rate of Fire: Very Fast

Effective Range: Medium

Reload Time: N/A

Features: None

Strengths: Automatic fire

Weaknesses: This rifle overheats faster than the Elite version.

Details: This weapon appears in the single player campaign. It is a variation of the Plasma Rifle wielded by Brutes. It is red in color and fires faster than the version used by Elites.

Plasma Sword

Dual Wield: Sadly, no.

Clip Size: N/A

Ammo Limit: N/A

Rate of Fire: Slow for lunge, medium for non-lunge swipe.

Effective Range: Short

Reload Time: N/A

Features: Lunge with target tracking.

Strengths: The lunge attack is lethal.

Weaknesses: Obviously, this blade only works up close.

Details: This weapon would probably win the award for coolest new addition to the Halo arsenal. If you have played Halo 1, then you have seen this weapon, but now you have the option of carrying it.

For a one hit fight, wait for the reticle to turn red and then pull the trigger. You will lunge forward and uppercut your target so hard that he will probably fly away from you. You can lunge higher than you would normally be able to jump.

Another option is to hack away at targets when you aren't locked onto them. Although you won't get frags as quickly, you also won't be as vulnerable as you would if you missed a lunge. You may want to try both techniques; so far I have found that the time it takes to recover from a missed lunge is not enough to outweigh the potential benefit of the quick one hit take down.

The impressive Plasma Sword.

Needler

Dual Wield: Yes

Clip Size: 30

Ammo Limit: 90

Rate of Fire: Fash

Effective Range: Medium

Reload Time: Medium

Features: Target tracking and some splash damage. Needles bounce off oblique angles so you could use this weapon for some sneaky ricochet attacks.

Strengths: Explosive needles.

Weaknesses: Needles move slower than other types of ammunition and they take a few seconds to explode. This gives your target a little bit of time to duck behind cover.

Details: I heard a Halo 2 player say that hitting someone with the Needler is "like hitting him with a wet sock." But I defend this often-maligned weapon because the Needler can be useful in Halo 2 when combined with another gun or dual wielding two of them.

The most effective feature of the Needler is that the Covenant shards will track your target. You can easily turn your opponent into a pin cushion if you catch him out in the open. Just be sure to get out of his firing line while you wait for the crystal shards to explode.

The Needler's homing feature's interesting side effect is that you can use the Needler to find opponents. If someone is hiding in the shadows, you may be able to discover their location by firing off a few shards.

Winning Tactic:

Try using two Needlers against opponents in the open courtyard of Lockout. And make sure that you can take cover after you unload!

The Covenant Needler.

Covenant Carbine

Dual Wield: No

Clip Size: 18

Ammo Limit: 72

Rate of Fire: Semi-automatic when zoomed, automatic without the scope.

Effective Range: Long

Reload Time: Medium

Features: Scope (2X)

Strengths: Flexible weapon at mid-range. Headshot bonus.

Weaknesses: No burst mode so it isn't well suited for close combat.

Details: The Carbine is the Covenant's answer to the Battle Rifle. In general, you can use it in much the same way as you would the human version, except that Covenant Carbine is semi-automatic whereas the Battle Rifle only fires bursts.

I love to harass the other team with this weapon when playing defense on Midship. It has a 2X scope so it's great for supporting my teammates who are going on the offensive.

The Covenant Carbine.

Particle Beam Rifle

Dual Wield: No

Clip Size: 100 (roughly 18 bursts)

Ammo Limit: N/A

Rate of Fire: Medium

Effective Range: Long

Reload Time: N/A (plasma weapon)

Features: Dual setting scope (5X and 10X)

Strengths: Powerful weapon with a headshot bonus and a scope.

Weaknesses: Overloads after a few shots.

Details: This is the Covenant's primary sniper tool, but it has a slightly different feel than the zoom option for the human version. Some people prefer the zoom on the Covenant weapon. In the single player campaign, the legendary Jackals are deadly with this weapon.

As with other plasma weapons, it will overheat. Make sure you give it time to cool when you see it heating up.

The Beam Rifle.

Brute Shot

Dual Wield: No

Clip Size: 4

Ammo Limit: 12

Rate of Fire: Medium

Effective Range: Long

Reload Time: Very Slow

Features: Rounds will bounce and they cause some splash damage.

Strengths: Powerful rounds.

Weaknesses: Slow reload time and a small clip. It is usually tough to get because it is one of the most powerful weapons.

Details: This is an interesting weapon to use. It fires bouncing projectiles so it takes a little bit of practice to understand. The Brute Shot can be very powerful when you use it correctly. Make use of the bouncing rounds by firing them around corners at unsuspecting opponents.

As mentioned in Chapter 2, Basic Combat, don't make the mistake of thinking that the Brute Shot is another Rocket Launcher. The rounds of the Brute Shot don't have the same splash damage impact so they won't finish your targets off as quickly as a Rocket Launcher.

The Brute Shot.

Fuel Rod Gun

Dual Wield: No
Clip Size: 5
Ammo Limit: 25
Rate of Fire: Medium
Effective Range: Medium
Reload Time: Medium
Features: Scope (2X)
Strengths: Excellent damage.
Weaknesses: Slow to reload.
Details: This weapon is powerful but it is only available in the single player campaign.

The Fuel Rod Gun.

Plasma Grenades

Dual Wield: N/A
Clip Size: N/A
Ammo Limit: 4
Rate of Fire: Medium
Effective Range: Long
Reload Time: N/A
Features: This grenade will stick to some surfaces—including your opponents.

Strengths: The ability to stick an opponent with a Plasma Grenade is a huge benefit. It's tough to dodge something that's affixed to your helmet. In addition, these grenades work well against shields.

Weaknesses: As with pineapples, you can only carry up to four of these. It takes longer for a Plasma Grenade to detonate so your prey may have time to scurry away before it blows.

Details: The blast radius of these grenades will take down shields.

A Plasma Grenade.

Crew 116 Advice: Plasma Grenades

Sticking an opponent with a Plasma Grenade is great, but it doesn't happen that often. Plasma Grenades take longer than Frag Grenades to explode. The downside to this is that it's difficult to land a grenade that your opponent can't avoid. The upside is that you can stick a grenade in a spot so your opponent can't go there. You can land a Plasma Grenade between you and your opponent to prevent him from approaching you. While you have him frozen, you can back up and hit him with a ranged weapon.

—DJ 116

Covenant Shade Turret

Dual Wield: N/A

Clip Size: N/A

Ammo Limit: Infinite

Rate of Fire: Medium

Effective Range: Medium

Reload Time: N/A

Features: None

Strengths: Unlimited ammunition and it can be moved with grenades.

Weaknesses: Lack of cover and this gun is stationary while you are firing.

Details: An enjoyable aspect of these 'stationary' guns is that you can actually move them. Hitting them is one way to do it, but for real impact drop grenades under them. If you plant your grenades just right, you can blast the turret in a specific direction. Blasting around Shades guns in the single player campaign of Halo 1 could completely change the dynamic of a level. How many of you tried knocking one of these 'stationary' guns off the ledge that overlooked the first Covenant gravity lift?

In Halo 2 there is a truly stationary Covenant turret. As with the human turrets, these guns offer considerable firepower but little cover. Make sure you use this weapon under the right circumstances and not when you're getting multiple Plasma Grenades chucked at you.

The Covenant Shade Turret.

Sentinel Beam

Dual Wield: No

Clip Size: 100

Ammo Limit: N/A

Rate of Fire: Constant

Effective Range: Medium

Reload Time: N/A

Features: Energy beam that toasts your target.

Strengths: Excellent damage when beam is maintained on the target.

Weaknesses: The beam must be held on the target.

Details: This weapon seems to be the Forerunner's answer to a flamethrower. However, it's more focused than a primitive human weapon so it is reasonable at range. Halo 1 players would have seen the Sentinels use this weapon against the Flood.

Unlike other Halo weapons, this one requires that you constantly hold the beam on the target. This makes the beam hard to use on its own.

The Sentinel Beam.

Chapter 4: Vehicles

Halo 1 included some exciting vehicle options. I am happy to say that Halo 2 has raised the bar. Not only have the developers at Bungie carried forward the enjoyable mayhem of vehicle combat, but they have also added features such as jacking and more vehicle destruction.

There are some changes to the Halo 1 vehicles and there are some new vehicles for you to enjoy. As with hand-held weapons, the vehicles have also gone through some changes based on overall balance. For example, the Scorpion tank no longer allows passengers to ride on its treads. This change balances the power of the main gun by rendering it more susceptible to infantry and jacking attacks.

Vehicles can easily determine the outcome of a game.

Human Vehicles

M12 Warthog LRV

Weaponry: Three-barreled machine gun.

Strengths: It moves quickly. It can carry up to three people—possibly even transporting a passenger with the flag.

Weaknesses: One rocket can take out the vehicle and all of its occupants. There is little cover for players in the jeep.

Crew: Driver, passenger, and gunner.

Features: Rear-mounted weapon for a gunner, an e-brake, and the crowd pleasing horn.

Supported On: Burial Mounds, Coagulation, Headlong, Waterworks, Zanzibar.

Details: The Warthog LRV (Light Reconnaissance Vehicle) is probably the vehicle that you will see the most in Halo 2 multiplayer games. It has the advantages of being able to carry three people (including the flag carrier—if allowed in the game settings) and move quickly. If you are able to get the flag carrier into a Warthog, it's extremely difficult for the defense to stop your team from getting a cap.

To best protect the gunner, you should almost always fire the Warthog gun forward. Not only are the guys in front of the vehicle the ones that can nade the jeep, but the Warthog gunner can also get cover from the chain gun. In addition, players behind your moving jeep will be getting progressively farther away whereas the players in front of you will be getting closer.

In Halo 1, it was best to fire short bursts from the Warthog's chain gun. In Halo 2, this still may be true but the spread is less so you may not need to worry about it. Also remember that if you're the passenger in a Warthog, you should carry plasma weapons so you can take down shields and let the chain gun work on bodies.

If you are playing the single player campaign, you will want to swap out injured marines if you find more healthy ones are in the area. This simply means that you always have the best possible force with you in the jeep.

The LRV Warthog.

The Warthog is also great for running over bodies—although it is now easier for your potential road kill to jump over you. Most people figured out that the best way to run someone over with the Halo 1 Warthog was to fishtail the back end as their victim tried to dodge to one side. Rumor has it that the Warthog 'E-brake' was added to enhance the fishtail effect. In Halo 2, this will likely still be the best way to run someone down. However, you'll have to make sure that you do it fast enough to avoid a jacking attempt.

One other thing to keep in mind is that the Warthog rolls more easily than most vehicles. The new Warthog is more stable but considering that Halo 2 vehicles take battle damage, you should still be careful about running into things – other players and monsters aren't an issue. When the vehicle rolls, you will likely fall out and there is also a chance that the jeep will land on you. Definitely don't run into Covenant fusion cores, the resulting blast will probably destroy you and your ride.

A Warthog in action.

Stopping a Warthog

A well-placed grenade used to be able to stop any jeep run. In Halo 2, you will probably have to use two. The reason for this is that the Halo 2 Warthog is harder to roll than the Halo 1 version. It used to be that a single grenade would likely flip the jeep and spill its occupants. In Halo 2 it is harder to do this. With the new homing option, rockets are definitely the best way to stop vehicles.

Stopping a Warthog.

M12G1 Warthog LAAV

Weaponry: Gauss Cannon.

Strengths: Designed to destroy vehicles; ability to transport a flag carrier.

Weaknesses: Occupants are not undercover; the gun has no splash damage.

Crew: Driver, passenger, and gunner.

Features: Same as M12 Warthog.

Supported On: Same as M12 Warthog.

Details: This vehicle is the same as the other Warthog except that it has a different weapon mounted on the back. The M12G1 is a light anti-armor vehicle (LAAV); the cannon on this special Warthog is designed to be used against vehicles.

The Gauss Warthog.

Crew 116 Advice: Warthog Cornering

The e-brake is your friend. It greatly improves your ability to take corners quickly.

—MrJukes

The Gauss Warthog cornering well.

M808B Scorpion Main Battle Tank

Weaponry: Main gun and machine gun.

Strength: Massive damage from the main gun shells.

Weaknesses: This tank is very slow moving. The turret can't fire above or below certain angles, although this seems to have been improved since Halo 1. The main gun is slow to load. Opponents can open the tank's hatch and attack the driver.

Crew: Driver only.

Features: Two weapons.

Supported On: Burial Mounds, Coagulation, Headlong, Waterworks, Zanzibar.

Details: The Scorpion can be so devastating that it completely changes the dynamic of any game. The main turret is one of the most powerful blasts in the entire game—only the Wraith mortar attack causes comparable damage.

When you're in this battle tank, you should focus on eliminating any opposition vehicles such as Wraiths or other Scorpions. Once you have those out of the way, you're free to move about the level—albeit rather slowly.

Try to set up the tank so that it's extremely difficult to snipe the driver from the front. Just like in Halo 1, you park facing away from your target and then turn the turret around. This is good for setting up a siege. Keeping the tank mobile is also important because sitting still is a death wish.

A Scorpion Tank.

Your main vulnerabilities are the tank's lack of speed, its inability to fire in all directions, and the fact that infantry can hijack your ride. Make sure you don't ignore players who try to approach on foot. The only reason that a player will do this is to open the tank's hatch. In addition, a well-piloted Banshee will be able to attack with impunity if the pilot keeps her craft directly above you.

When opening the hatch of a Scorpion, you have a couple of options. Once you have boarded the tank, you can chuck a grenade into the driver's compartment or you can simply melee the poor guy at the controls.

As previously mentioned, the Scorpion no longer supports passengers. A few possible reasons for this change jump to mind. The fact that there are no shooters on the treads means that infantry have a decent chance at getting to the tank's hatch; however, the most likely reason is that having passengers was only useful in the single player campaign. In multiplayer, the passengers were usually sitting ducks. In Halo 1, a Scorpion that got hit with a full complement of passengers just meant more frags for the other team. Another issue was that the passengers had severely limited vision and aiming ability.

Stopping a Scorpion: It takes many rockets to destroy a tank; even killing the driver is not likely with a single rocket. If you have to stop a tank without rockets, your best bet is probably to open the hatch and drop a grenade. Remember that the Scorpion cannot fire straight up so attacking with a Banshee can protect you from the tank's fire.

Crew 116 Advice: Scorpion

Be mindful of what is on the ground around you. If somebody gets in too close, you won't be able to shoot him anymore. You'll have to either run him over or bail.

—MrJukes

On a Scorpion.

A disabled Scorpion.

Covenant Vehicles

Ghost

Weaponry: Plasma cannons.

Strengths: Speed and the ability to strafe.

Weakness: Driver is not covered.

Crew: Driver only.

Features: Speed burst through a boosted gravity propulsion drive.

Supported On: Burial Mounds, Coagulation, Headlong, Waterworks, Zanzibar.

Details: The Ghost is a fast reconnaissance and assault vehicle. If you need to get from one place to another, this vehicle is probably the fastest way for you to get there on the ground.

The new speed burst feature of the Ghost is useful, but it comes with disadvantages. When you are using the speed burst, you compromise maneuverability. With this in mind, it's best to line up your path and then punch the overdrive. In addition, when you are using the speed burst, you will not be able to fire the Ghost's dual cannons.

As with other vehicles, you can use the Ghost to run over opponents. The Ghost's ability to strafe means that you can target infantry and dodge incoming fire. Strafing with the Ghost is also useful against the larger vehicles. Because the Ghost is so agile, you can quickly circle around a Scorpion or a Wraith. The other vehicle simply won't be able to turn fast enough to fire on you.

Stopping a Ghost: The speed burst makes it hard to grenade a Ghost and more challenging to jack. Your best bet is to use a locked-on rocket or wait for them to try to run you over. As the Ghost approaches, you can attempt to jack it or jump over it. One change that you should keep in mind is that it is more difficult to duck a Ghost than it was in Halo 1.

A Ghost.

Crew 116 Advice: Fighting Infantry with a Ghost

Running opponents over is fun, but the safest way to get a Ghost kill is to shoot them. Ideally, you want to avoid nades by strafing around your opponent in a circle.

—DJ 116

Dodge this...

Crew 116 Advice: Ghost.

If you are going to run over someone, make sure you turbo into him. You cannot get jacked while using the turbo.

—MrJukes

A Ghost using its speed burst.

Banshee

Weaponry: Plasma cannons (and Fuel Rod Cannon in the single player campaign mode).

Strengths: The Banshee is the only airborne vehicle in the game, and it is difficult to jack.

Weakness: Vulnerable to guided rockets.

Crew: Driver only.

Features: Evasive roll.

Supported On: Ascension, Coagulation, Headlong, Waterworks, Zanzibar.

Details: The Banshee is the only flying vehicle that you can control. Use this fact to your advantage by launching 'shock and awe' campaigns against powerful terrestrial vehicles. For example, if you maneuver above the Scorpion or the Wraith, you have the freedom to bombard them from an angle that they cannot attack.

One obvious change is that the Halo 2 Banshee is not a 'sky turret'. In other words, the hover feature is gone. This makes it more difficult to keep your reticle on your target. Many Halo 1 players have fond memories of hovering above a battlefield during the single player campaign. While it is true that you won't be able to stay on target as easily as you could before, you can remain on target by using well-timed rolls.

When piloting the Banshee, ensure that you avoid crashing into objects. This will damage the craft and ultimately shorten your flight time. In addition, don't forget that the lack of falling damage means that you can essentially parachute out of the Banshee. For example, on the Coagulation map you could fly above the other team's base and drop yourself down. I'm sure that most players wouldn't expect an ODST move pulled on them.

A Banshee.

A Banshee raining down on a Scorpion.

Crew 116 Advice: Banshee Piloting

Never fly in a straight line. You never know when a rocket is bearing down on you. You are in a flying machine; there is no reason to be skimming the ground. Try to get high above them and rain down death and destruction without remorse. The primary gun is nice to lay down cover fire. If you have to face a Banshee, try to stay in a covered area. The reasonable ways to take down a Banshee are with the Rocket Launcher, a tank, or another Banshee.

—MrJukes

Stopping a Banshee: A couple of locked-on rockets is your best bet. It's tough to take down a Banshee if the pilot is paying attention and has dodging skills. You might want to find your own Banshee and have a dogfight.

If you're feeling particularly gusty, you can try to jack a Banshee. It is possible, but you might have to put your life on the line so practice with a buddy before you attempt it in a ranked hopper.

I sure hope this works!

Spectre

Weaponry: Rear-mounted plasma cannon.

Strength: Speed burst.

Weakness: Light armor.

Crew: Driver and gunner.

Feature: Speed burst.

Supported On: Burial Mounds, Coagulation, Headlong, Waterworks, Zanzibar.

Details: This vehicle is sort of like the love child of the Warthog and the Ghost. A gunner can fire a rear-mounted weapon, like the Warthog, but it also comes with the Ghost's ability to strafe.

Stopping a Spectre: To stop this machine, use the same tricks that you would use against a Ghost or Warthog.

Having some fun with a new toy.

The Spectre.

Wraith Tank

Weaponry: Plasma mortar.

Strengths: Very powerful plasma cannon; speed burst.

Weaknesses: Weak armor; main gun cannot fire straight up or down; weapon is slow to recharge; plasma mortar moves relatively slowly.

Crew: Driver only.

Features: Speed burst.

Supported On: Burial Mounds, Coagulation, Headlong, Waterworks, Zanzibar.

Details: The Wraith was a fun opponent in the Halo 1 campaign. In Halo 2, you have the option of operating this impressive machine. The Wraith mortar attack is one of the most powerful weapons in the game. However, just like the Scorpion, the Wraith pays for this power with its lack of maneuverability.

The Wraith does have one distinct advantage over the Scorpion tank; it features a short speed burst. Although it doesn't last long, it is enough to win a race against a human tank.

Stopping a Wraith: Fighting against a Wraith is similar to taking on a Scorpion. However, the Wraith is harder to jack because of its speed boost capability. The good news is that the Wraith doesn't have a machine gun like the Scorpion. This makes it easier for you to get in close—just hope that the driver doesn't notice you and turbo away.

Wraith Tank.

Now what?

The limited Wraith turbo is useful.

Vehicle Tactics and Techniques

Here are some general techniques for using the Halo 2 weapons. One thing to note is that the smaller vehicles are fairly easy to pick off with large weapons. For example, the Halo 2 rocket homing feature is deadly to vehicles. Because of this, players tend to use small vehicles for fast transport instead of as weapons. This is especially true on the larger maps.

The exception to this is the Puma when the rear gun is manned by a teammate. The combination of the maneuverability of the Warthog and its weapon make it a powerful enough force that it is worth risking a rocket in the chops.

Destructible Vehicles

The biggest vehicle change for Halo 1 fans is the fact that many vehicles now can be destroyed. It is important to recognize that this will have an effect on strategy. For example, if your game settings allow flag carriers to jump into the Warthog, you will want your jeep in one piece when the flag carrier runs out with the other team's cloth. If your Warthog is still in one piece, you will have a chance to chauffeur the flag back to your base. Although vehicles will eventually re-spawn after they have been destroyed, you will want to ensure that they are mobile when you need them.

Also, you have to be wary of secondary explosions. After you have abandoned a fatally damaged vehicle, make sure that you're out of the blast zone. Ghosts seem to have the most dangerous secondary explosion because their parts have a tendency to fly around more than the other types of vehicle wreckage. After some time, the vehicle will reappear in its spawn location.

Wreckage of a Warthog.

Vehicle Suicides

Deaths caused by vehicles carry the same re-spawn penalty as a suicide. Therefore, you may be able to force a long re-spawn by jumping out of a vehicle just as it coasts over your target. Instead of being credited with a frag, your foe will be charged with a suicide. If you're behind in a slayer game, this will drop your opponent's score and could give your team a little bit more time to catch up—not to mention bragging rights for a sweet move.

Let it roll.

Jacking

Vehicle hijacking, or jacking, can be accomplished when you are close to a slow moving vehicle, or when you have boarded a vehicle by jumping onto it. There are slight variations for some vehicles but the general idea is that you hold down the 'X' button and switch places with the driver. Not only will you have control of the vehicle, but you will certainly confuse your opponent for a short period of time. This may be all you need to shift the conflict in your favor.

Crew 116 Advice: Jacking

You don't have to hit 'X' at the exact right moment. You can just hold it down and when a vehicle gets close enough, you will board it.

—MrJukes

Note

Vehicle hijacking is an outstanding addition to the Halo game engine. The program manager who was able to get this feature in the box deserves some sort of award. In addition, the execution of the coding and animation are brilliant—so basically the whole feature crew deserves some hardware for this one.

It may take some practice before you're able to jack vehicles. Don't give up though—when you do it, it will be so rewarding. Not only is it a great way to stick it to another player, but it can also be a huge shift in the game's struggle for power.

For example, my first successful jacking came at the best possible moment. I consider myself lucky to have pulled this off, but it has supported my belief that jacking is a skill worth the time it takes to learn. It was a CTF game on Zanzibar and the other team had infiltrated the base. The flag carrier ran out of the open gate and hopped into a waiting Warthog. Fortunately, I was on the top level of the base—right above the jeep. I jumped down as an opponent hopped into the driver's seat. I pressed the 'X' button and yanked the poor guy right out. I'll never forget the instant that the flag carrier looked over and discovered that the driver was the wrong color. Even through the MJOLNIR, I could tell that his jaw had dropped. By successfully jacking that Puma, I believe that I saved a cap.

If you're driving a vehicle around, you must remember that any player who gets close enough is a potential car-jacker. Even if you're in the Scorpion or the Wraith, be sure that you don't ignore infantry. If you're in the Ghost, you may want to prevent jacking by using the speed burst when you pass by enemies.

Crew 116 Advice: Banshee Jacking

Banshee jacking can be a blast. There is nothing better than jumping off the edge of a cliff in the hope of hijacking a Banshee. You either make it or fall to your death. If you are able to jack the Banshee, you can send your enemy plummeting. When you are getting jacked out of a Banshee, hold down 'X'. Most of the time you can re-jack the Banshee before you lose your ride.

—MrJukes

One consequence of the new jacking feature is something affectionately known as 'the never-ending jack.' This happens when you re-jack the vehicle that you have just lost. You can do this by holding down the 'X' key while you are being jacked. However, if the other person does the same thing, then he can jack it back. When you are jacking a Ghost, breaking this cycle often requires that you use the speed boost to get away from the opponent.

Jacking a Ghost.

Chauffeuring the Flag

Getting the flag into a Warthog is a huge CTF advantage. However, you will need two players to pull it off since another player must act as the chauffer because the flag carrier cannot drive. On a map like Zanzibar, it is extremely difficult to stop a cap once the flag is being carried in a Warthog. For this reason, it is definitely worth your while to try to coordinate a Warthog arrival as the flag carrier leaves the enemy base.

This tactic requires teamwork and communication. The best way to pull off this move is to talk about it before you get the flag. Remember that your other teammates can run interference. As the flag starts to move, stage a frontal assault and tie up any forces that could prevent the flag carrier from getting to the jeep. If you find that the other team is coordinated enough to have a rocket defense against your jeep assault, then make sure that you have a sniper ready to target the rocket position.

A quick getaway with the cloth.

Chapter 5: Advanced Combat

Chapter 2, Basic Combat, introduced you to Halo 2 battle tactics. Now that you've mastered the basics, you are ready to build on those skills by tackling the advanced techniques used by expert Halo 2 gamers.

The most important skill a Halo 2 player possesses is the ability to assess the situation and employ the appropriate tactic. You will naturally develop your own favorite technique that will serve you well in many situations, but this can become dangerously limiting. Resist the temptation to force your favorite technique onto every situation. Practice these advanced combat tactics to determine which ones best complement your playing style.

The tactics described in this section are not bugs in the game; these are tried and true methods of improving your performance in Halo 2 battles. Regardless of whether you are fighting against Halo AI opponents, or against someone next to you on the couch, these techniques will empower you to reach your full potential as a Halo 2 player.

Grenades

The jury is in. The proper use of grenades is definitely an art. Expert players don't just throw grenades around and hope for the best, they use them for specific purposes. In addition to grenade jumping and using grenades to blast objects around, here are some other ways to use 'nades.

In Halo 1, there were many cases where you could maneuver a creature near a drop-off. Once you had the alien in position, you could simply chuck a grenade to the opposite side of the cliff. This gives the target the option of moving toward the cliff or taking damage from the grenade. In their attempts to get out of the way, many aliens would inadvertently jump to their demise. While you may not be able to get fellow multiplayer combatants to commit a suicide, you can certainly trap them in places where they are vulnerable to a well-placed 'nade. For example, if you know that someone is camping, you can use a grenade to soften him up before you charge his position.

You also should use grenades to move players around the map. Dependant upon your current weapon load, you may want your targets to move closer to you or farther away from you. Throwing a grenade just behind a player will move him toward you, whereas throwing a grenade in front of someone will force him to move back. If opponents ignore these grenade moves, then they will be subject to damage—either way you end up better off.

In the heat of battle, don't forget that you can use grenades both offensively and defensively. For example, if an enemy is pursuing you, simply turn a bit and bounce a grenade off a wall. This way you can throw a grenade— without turning completely around— so it lands behind you.

Drop grenades as you retreat.

Although it may be slightly more difficult than in Halo 1, short hopping is still a very valuable skill. The fuse for fragmentation grenades will start as soon as they hit the ground, so dropping one right next to you is the fastest way to set off a pineapple. This tactic will either buy you some extra time as you retreat or weaken your attacker. Given the choice, some players disengage after being blasted with a grenade.

Crew 116 Advice: Short-Hopping Grenades

In Halo 1, frag grenades blew up shortly after stopping. In Halo 2, they blow up about half a second after hitting the floor for the first time. This new behavior makes it harder to short-hop a grenade and get it to blow up early.

—*char*

Most Halo 1 players also learned in the single player campaign that a bunch of grenades on the ground could act as a brutal booby trap. If you know that there is a cluster of grenades on the ground, all you have to do is add a live one and you will trigger a chain reaction. In this way, grenades on the ground can be treated like discarded Covenant fusion cores.

Drop a grenade when your opponent is cornered.

Crew 116 Advice: Grenades

You can't fire when you are throwing a grenade. Most beginners throw grenades too often and at the wrong times. If you waste too much time throwing grenades that miss your target, you will be an easy kill for someone who fires at you the entire time. The best strategy is to get momentary cover while you throw your grenade. If you can use a map object to block line of sight for just a moment, you can throw a grenade without losing crucial fighting time.

—*DJ 116*

Plasma Grenades

Use Plasma Grenades primarily to knock out enemy shields. The splash damage from a Plasma Grenade can completely drain a healthy target's shielding. If you see a cluster of enemies, chuck a Plasma Grenade into their midst. Unless they scatter, you could take out a bunch of shields.

Fragmentation Grenades

Fragmentation Grenades are most useful against bodies. If you're trying the short-hop move against a pursuer, use one of these pineapples. Not only do they detonate more quickly, but they allow you to save your Plasma Grenades for use against shields.

Grenade Jumping and Rocket Jumping

Jumping with the help of grenades and rockets is a pretty cool trick. The principle is straightforward: you use the power of a grenade or rocket to propel yourself into the air. Using this method you are able to jump higher than you can with the 'A' button. Even though people have been doing this since the time of Quake®, it is still fun and effective.

Rocket jumping is a bit tougher than grenade jumping because you are more likely to punch your own ticket in the attempt. However, it's just a matter of timing. With some practice, you can add both methods to your game. It's best to try this trick when you have an Overshield. Without extra protection, you can count on your shields being knocked out.

While it may seem that this is just a foolhardy way to lose your shields, the extra height that you get from these jumps can be a strategic advantage. Sometimes, you may decide that it's worth the risk. As you run around the multiplayer levels, you should be looking for chances to use this technique. If you find a nice jump, you will probably have ample opportunity to sneak up on unsuspecting prey. Just remember that you will want to recharge your shields after the jump; ideally, you don't want to land next to an enemy. If you have a comrade with you, one can make the jump and secure the landing zone and then when the other follows, you can make a surprise entrance together.

Grenade jumping on Lockout.

Blasting Objects to You

The Halo 2 engine is a remarkable creation. For example, gamers can manipulate objects in the game in ways they used to only dream about. Other games may have laid the foundation for this technology but Halo 2 has taken game physics to a new level. Blasting around weapons and powerups is one example of using the Halo 2 engine.

Instead of wasting your precious time running around collecting your weapons, find ways to manipulate the engine in your favor. If you're familiar with Halo 1's Hang 'em High level, then you might know that the Rocket Launcher and Sniper Rifle could both be grabbed from a considerable distance. All it took was a couple of well-aimed grenade tosses.

Over time, Halo fans will find all sorts of interesting ways to blast things around the Halo 2 maps. It will be interesting to see what happens with the new vehicle explosions. Will teams find ways to use the new Halo 2 features to move objects to their position? Check your favorite Halo 2 websites for updates.

A great example of blasting a weapon in Halo 2 is the Zanzibar Plasma Sword. A precise grenade will free the sword from its alcove and allow you to pick it up from the bottom of the wheel.

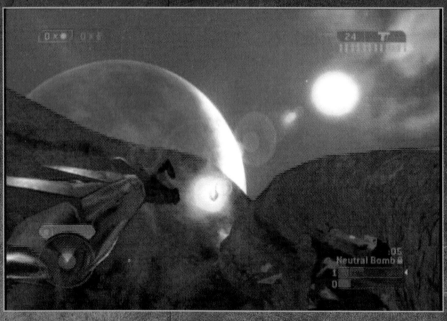

Lining up a grenade to capture a weapon.

Shields

You will spend most of your time fighting against shielded opponents during Halo 2 games. Obviously, this includes the single player campaign. Now that the health bar is gone, shields are even more important. When engaging a shielded opponent, you should remember these principles:

1. **Use plasma weapons against shields.**

2. **Use projectile weapons against bodies.**

3. **Since the Mark VI armor has a faster recharge time, you will need to be more aggressive when you manage to drop an enemy's shield. Don't give your opponent time to recharge her shields.**

Use plasma against shields.

Rumor has it that the health system was changed so that people won't get stuck with trifling health in tough sections of the single player campaign. If this is true, it's a bitter pill for Halo 2 multiplayer fans to swallow. However, one has to remember that the good people at Bungie know what they are doing. They undoubtedly had data from gamers that compelled them to make this change.

Just keep in mind that minimizing the importance of health—and improving the shield recharge time—effectively belittles a strategic element of Halo 1 multiplayer. Those of you who used health packs to sway battles will simply have to rely more heavily on other techniques. Making shields more important also makes plasma weapons more important. If you primarily used human weapons in Halo 1, you may want to make a change.

Find cover when your shield alarm goes off.

When your shield alarm is triggered, you should consider whether it's time to retreat. The great thing about the Halo 2 shields is that you can come back almost completely healed if you can just find cover and let your shields recharge.

Overshield

I can remember telling a friend over and over that he must use the Halo powerups. Eventually, he accepted the advice and now I have a hard time beating him. Making the most of every possible advantage is the prerogative of any player. Just like Striker of Crew 116 wrote in his bio, "If you've got something that's working for you, use it and abuse it."

Crew 116 Advice: Trumping a Battle

In any battle, the Overshield can be a "trump card."

—*Char*

You may feel that information about using the powerups could go into Chapter 2, Basic Combat. In a sense that is true. However, a lot of players don't use these tools well. Not only should you grab the powerups, you should make the most of them.

The Overshield is a prime example of an advantage that can easily sway the outcome of an otherwise close match up. If you have the Overshield, you should be aggressive. Remember that you have limited time so use your strengthened status to its full potential. Conversely, if you know that your opponent has the Overshield, then you must factor this into your decision about whether to engage or not.

If you have a Plasma Pistol, you can still have a fair fight with an Overshielded opponent. The overcharged plasma ball is the best answer to the Overshield. If you hit with the first ball, then you've negated the other gamer's advantage.

As soon as you collect the Overshield, there is a short charging time. During this time, you are invincible—except for a melee to the back of the head. You can use this small window as a perfect time for a grenade or rocket jump. Instead of compromising your shields, you have a free chance to make a quick high jump.

The Halo 2 Overshield.

Active Camouflage

Another Halo 2 powerup is the Active Camouflage. This pyramid renders the player almost invisible. It's very tough to see a player who is concealed with this powerup—especially in dark areas. Once you have collected this goodie, you have a limited amount of time before it wears off.

If you get the Active Camouflage, you should use it wisely. Don't just try to sneak up on the first opponent that you see. Think about your options. For example, is there some place that you would like to get to on the map? If you are playing a game where a certain weapon is being camped, this may be your chance to pick it up. If you are playing a team game, you may want to do some reconnaissance. In the single player campaign, it can help you discover traps that are in your path. In multiplayer games, you can report on the enemy's troop movements. This can be particularly useful in large team games. The situation will determine the best use of invisibility. Choose the application that best applies to your situation.

If you are playing an FFA match, you may want to use your hidden status to steal weapons from other players. This is another reason why you don't want to give away your location the first time that you see an opponent. Maybe there is someone close by with a better weapon to take. However, if you are playing on a small multiplayer map, and you feel that you are well armed, you may want to get into as many fights as possible before your camouflage time runs out.

The Halo 2 Active Camouflage.

On small maps, the Shotgun and Active Camouflage are a lethal combination. The invis allows you to get right next to targets and the Shotgun is a single shot weapon at short range.

Keep in mind that certain activities will break the invisibility affect. These include firing, driving, or running with the flag, ball, or bomb. If you fire a powerful weapon such as the Rocket Launcher, you will be immediately visible. However, if you fire a single round from an SMG, it will barely affect your visibility. Once you stop firing, the camouflage will gradually take effect again. This is just one more reason why you should choose your goal carefully when you pick up the active camouflage.

Three Weapon Tile Puzzle

Now that you can carry three weapons, make sure you make the most of your arsenal. Regardless of where a particular weapon happens to be, you can always move it to a different location. This technique works like a tile puzzle.

Imagine that you have a Magnum in your left hand, a Plasma Pistol in your right hand, and an SMG in your backpack. If you melee, you will drop your Magnum. Stand over the Magnum and use the 'X' button to drop the Plasma Pistol and pick the Magnum up again. This means that you have switched the Magnum from your left hand to your right.

Continuing on with this example, move away from the weapon at your feet and use the 'Y' button to switch to your SMG. Standing over the Plasma Pistol, use 'X' to drop the SMG and pick up the Plasma Pistol, and then use 'Y' to dual wield the SMG that you just dropped. Now you have changed the position of all three guns. You are dual wielding the SMG with the Magnum and the Plasma Pistol is in your backpack.

Although it takes time to switch weapons around, the tile puzzle movement will be especially useful in the single player campaign. Having the right combo out at the right time will mean that you're using your arsenal to its full potential.

In addition, if you're a lefty, you might want to switch your favorite weapon to your left hand. I'm left handed but I don't find that this is important enough for me to bother with; however, I encourage you to try it and make your own decision.

Using Your Settings

In the spirit of using every possible element to your advantage, don't forget to find the controller settings that work best for your style. Play around with different options and find the specific configuration that will bring out the best in your play. The following are several important setting considerations.

The Halo 2 settings screen.

Look Sensitivity

Of all your profile settings, this is probably the most important. Adjust your look sensitivity so that it is as high as possible while not adversely affecting your accuracy. You may want to try playing at different speeds. This will help you find the setting that is right for you.

In addition, you may want to change your look sensitivity based on the game type that you will be playing. For example, when playing shotguns, I like to have my sensitivity set at 10 so that I can turn quickly and get off the first shot. However, when using long-range weapons, it's easier to aim if you have your sensitivity turned down. Snipers generally like to keep their sensitivity level lower than most players do. However, the snipers to fear the most are the ones who are still deadly with their look sensitivity high.

Color

Since it is an advantage to be hidden, you might want to consider a low profile color.

On dark maps, the darker colors might give you a distinct advantage. However, on lighter maps, you may want to choose white or steel. Most people use the color setting to express themselves. There is nothing wrong with that but remember that your color can also be used as camouflage.

Maybe not.

When you think about it, it's a bit strange that the two colors for Halo 1 teams were red and blue. I always wondered why they chose red when that color is so obvious on most maps. However, that's all academic now that Halo 2 supports many more team colors. You will only be limited to red and blue on system link games.

Screen Brightness

Interestingly enough, your screen brightness settings can help your game. If you take the time to set up your monitor or television properly, you will be able to see the battlefield better. I didn't think that this was such a big deal until I happened to be playing through a VGA connector one day. Switching between the monitor and the TV, I noticed a big difference when it came to dark areas of the maps. On the monitor screen, I could simply see more than I could see on the other.

Check your brightness settings and experiment to find the configuration that allows you to see the most of the map. I recommend that you do this on a dark map. For example, Waterworks would be an excellent candidate for checking your brightness.

Button Setup

Go into the controller settings options and try some of the other layouts. You might find one that better suits your game than the default layout. Playing Halo 2 on the Xbox might not offer you the same freedom as Halo PC controller mappings, but there are still significant changes that you can make.

For example, many players are big fans of the 'Boxer' configuration. In this layout, the right thumbstick push gesture is your melee attack. Halo 1 players liked this because it decreased the effect of an accidental push. If you were carrying a weapon with a scope, you would normally zoom in when your right thumbstick is pressed. Instead of finding yourself recovering from a mistake, you could potentially cause damage with your error. However, this isn't the only reason that people use the Boxer configuration. Some people just like the fact that the melee is available without taking your thumb off the thumbstick.

Using Your Ears

While sight is obviously the most important sense in a Halo 2 match, don't forget that your ears can also give you an advantage. Halo 2 supports positional Dolby Digital 5.1 surround sound. This means that a good sound setup can also be an advantage. There should be times when you'll be able to tell 'where' a sound originated.

Pay attention to the sounds that you hear around you. Explosions will reveal other players' positions and indicate where fights are happening. If you're close to a powerup, you should be able to hear if someone else has stolen it before you. This can be enough for you to decide to make a fast retreat. For example, you usually don't want to take on someone who just picked up an Overshield.

Using Timers

In the Halo 2 universe, many items have regular spawn intervals, and some smart players use timers so they can be prepared when something is about to appear. Players start the timer at the beginning of a game so they will know when each of the items on the maps will reappear based on the elapsed time. For example, the rockets might appear every two minutes. If the player notices that the Rocket Launcher is gone, he simply needs to go back to the spot when enough time has elapsed.

Tip

Check the Internet for published lists of re-spawn times for items.

You can imagine that if you're playing team games, you might have one timer for the people on the offensive box and another for the defensive box. That way only one person keeps track of the timer and can easily notify his teammates when something important is about to appear close to them.

Snipers

If you enjoy getting up close and personal with your enemy, then the Halo 2 sniper weapons probably aren't right for you. On the other hand, if you're a good shot and enjoy supporting your team, sniping with long range weapons like the human Sniper Rifle or the new Covenant Beam Rifle could be just the type of work that suits your playing style.

In team games, the sniper weapons are reserved for the player who accepts the Midfield role. Snipers don't typically score a lot of points in team games. However, they often have a high kill total at the end of the game. The reason for this is that the sniper is primarily responsible for suppression fire. The sniper is there to support her team whether the enemy is advancing or defending. For more about team roles, see Chapter 7, Team Strategy.

Make the First Shot Count

Firing the sniper weapons are some of the most obvious shots in the game. You must be cognizant of the fact that your first shot is unique. After that first shot, your target will know that you are firing at him. In addition, the beam or contrail effect will tell him exactly where you are perched.

This is particularly important when you are playing against other snipers. In top-level games, the snipers are deadly. If you don't get one with the first shot, don't expect him to miss.

Choose Your Perch Carefully

When setting up your sniper spot, make sure that you have considered all of the important factors. However, don't expect to find a position that renders you immovable. The Bungie level designers try hard to create levels that are fair for all types of players. This means that snipers should not be able to camp out and ignore attackers.

Obviously, your objective will determine the view that you're hoping to find. If you are assigned to guard your own base, then you need to see as many of the ingress paths as possible. However, if your goal is midfield suppression, then you need to be able to see as many paths as possible in both directions.

Your vulnerability is another important consideration when sniping. Obviously, you want to have

as much cover as possible. However, if you can best deal with your objective without cover, then you may choose to do so. For example, if you're after a flag carrier, you may choose to compromise your security by high tailing it after her.

Ideally, you want to be somewhere high that offers cover and at least two exit paths. This will give you the best view and the best security. If an attacker cuts off one escape route, you can use the other to get away.

Choose Your Targets More Carefully

Since your first shot is the most important, save it for the most important target. If you see a couple of potential victims, take the time to figure out which shot will best serve to further your objective. For more about prioritizing your targets, see Chapter 6, Solo Strategy.

Your Clip

Most weapons give you plenty of chances to hit your target. The human Sniper Rifle is not one of these weapons. You only get four shots before you have to reload, which is yet another reason that you must be smart when choosing your shots. If you're using the Covenant Beam Rifle, you will get more total rounds but you still can't fire them very fast. The overheating of the Beam Rifle results in an effective clip size that is similar to the human Sniper Rifle.

Try not to overheat the Beam Rifle.

Four rounds is not a large clip. You should expect that the player in your sights is counting your rounds. When you fire that fourth shot, he will know that it's safe for his getaway.

Let's say that you have a player pinned behind a rock. You don't have a good shot and your opponent is baiting you by short strafing so that he just sticks out a bit every time. Rather than fire off all four of your rounds, leave him there. Since you have essentially frozen the player and he is not an immediate threat, you are free to quickly scan for other targets. If the player thinks that you've moved, he may choose to make a break for cover. As you scan back to him, you will find that you now have a good shot.

Now that's a sniper perch!

Night Vision

When you are in the single player campaign and you have the human Sniper Rifle, don't forget about the night vision scope. Even if you aren't planning to take a shot, the scope can reveal important aspects of the battlefield.

Aim Using the Sniper Rifles

The sniper weapons offer the best scope magnification in the game. This translates to the best zoom if you're looking at things and also the best aiming tool for other weapons. If you are going to fire off a rocket at a distant target, use the Sniper Rifle or the Beam Rifle to aim and then switch to the Rocket Launcher. If you fire without moving your reticle, your shot will have the same accuracy as a Sniper Rifle bullet.

The sniper scope is also invaluable for reconnaissance. If your team needs a quick scouting report, the sniper scope is the best tool for the job.

Using Vehicles

Make it more difficult for other players to get to you by having a getaway vehicle nearby. Snipers attract a lot of attention and other players will try their hardest to get to your perch. If you have a vehicle waiting nearby, it gives you other options when someone approaches.

The first option is simply to bug out. You can cover ground far more quickly using a vehicle than on foot. The second option is to engage the attacker with the vehicle. If the enemy is approaching on foot, you can surprise him by quickly switching from a sniper to a driver.

The Ghost is the fastest vehicle in the game so many people feel that it is the best option for supporting a sniper. Regardless of which vehicle you choose, try to keep it concealed until you make the decision to leave your sniper spot.

Look Sensitivity Reminder

Since the long range weapons are the most sensitive to your look sensitivity setting, make sure that your profile is adjusted properly. As already mentioned in this chapter, look sensitivity is a great way to improve your aiming skills. Snipers generally like to lower their sensitivity so that they can more easily make fine adjustments.

Playing Against a Sniper

Many people feel helpless against the surprise of being sniped. It is true that it's tough to avoid that first unexpected shot. However, once you are aware that a sniper is after you there are some things that you can do to improve your chances for survival.

Remember the Four Rounds

As already mentioned, one of the weaknesses of the human Sniper Rifle is its small clip size. Unlike most weapons, it's easy to keep track of the number of rounds in a sniper's clip. Once you see or hear those four shots fired, you're free to escape without further harassment. The sniper will have to reload before he can take another shot at you.

Evasion

If a sniper is hunting you, you must get behind cover as fast as possible. If you're facing the human Sniper Rifle, make sure that you don't get pinned down and give him another four shots. When at all possible, you should run toward the cover that will give you an escape route. In other words, don't just run behind the closest rock. Think of it this way, the sniper has already fired at you, so you know that he only has three rounds left. Would you rather hide behind a rock and let the sniper reload? Then you would be facing four more shots. Generally, the best plan is to immediately run to an exit and only face three more.

Just stay still.

Closing In

You may decide that the best way to deal with an enemy sniper is to put him out of business. Your first option is to engage with ranged weapons. A rifle or a Rocket Launcher can make quick work of a sniper. However, if you don't happen to have a rifle or a rocket in your backpack, you have the option of rushing the sniper perch.

Keep in mind that if you rush the perch, you're running directly at a sniper; you are not evading. From your perspective, you are running at full speed but from the perspective of the sniper your orientation isn't changing that much. When you charge a sniper's position, make sure that you are strafing as well as moving forward. Ideally, you want to approach from a concealed location or use the active camouflage.

Once you are close enough, you can either engage with short range weapons or you can carpet bomb the sniper's location with grenades. Of course, the best plan might be to do both. First, soften the location with grenades, and then charge. If you have a strong short-range weapon, there is a good chance that you'll have an advantage against the sniper. Unless he has prepared for you, he may not have a short-range weapon that can compete with yours.

Crew 116 Advice: char's Guide to Sniping

If the rockets are a chainsaw, then the sniper is a scalpel. Use it to selectively remove opponents from the battlefield. The military calls snipers "force multipliers". There's an interesting article on www.howthingswork.com about snipers.

—char

Aiming
Lead your targets if they're really far away. In 10x zoom, it's almost always necessary. Practice this so that you're able to hit people at both zoom levels. Use the right one for the job.

Targeting
Shoot the guy who's the biggest threat to your team. That's often not the closest guy. If you're being shot at, either tag the opponent(s) or relocate. On offense, support the push. On defense, take out opponents near the base or endangering teammates. Control key positions and weapon spawns on the map. Don't let them get rockets or invis for example.

Don't waste sniper ammo on close range targets. Drop them with a shorter-range gun.

Perch
Personally, I prefer being mobile. The only time I'll perch is if I need a better view. I tend to avoid the obvious perches on the maps. Find a spot that players don't expect fire to come from, and that has a good view of the field. At the same time, ensure it's defensible so you can duck out of harm's way.

Sniper Defense
Get a rifle of your own and beat him at his game. If that's not possible, use cover or ports to close the distance. At range, he'll always win. Distract with a tasty target teammate and flank him while he's occupied. Alternatively, run him out of ammo.

Other Responsibilities
Since the sniper often has the best view of the field and the best zoom, scouting is an important secondary role. Additionally, having a good handle on what's critical to the goal is important—so you can shoot the right target. For these two reasons, the sniper can make a good team leader. Provide intel, support the goal, and help lead your team.

Covenant vs. Human Rifles
The Covenant Beam Rifle overheats at high fire rates. However, you can fire it slowly enough that it won't overheat. If you're good at headshots, I prefer the cov rifle, since you can keep it from overheating. The human rifle has four shots, and then it needs to reload. If you need more than two shots to kill a target, or have a lot of targets to neutralize in a short timespan, the human rifle is better.

Dual Weapon Combos

Dual wielding is not only a fun new feature, it's also a chance for you to show your intelligence on the battlefield. Just like any other tactic, you need to use the right tool for the right job.

Remember that reloading two guns is more complicated than a single weapon. You may want to hit reload on one while the other still has some ammo. This allows you to fire and reload at the same time. If you're caught with two empty clips, switch to your third weapon. Reloading two guns can take a long time.

Crew 116 Advice: Dual Weapons

In general, unless you're really happy with your grenades, you should grab a second weapon when you find yourself just holding a single dinky weapon. Trade up as you come across things (you can swap out either weapon with one on the floor by holding 'X' or 'Y' respectively).

—char

Unfortunately, you can't dual wield all weapons—but then again two Rocket Launchers wouldn't be all that sporting.

In Halo 2, the following are dual wielding weapons:

- Magnum Pistol
- SMG
- Plasma Pistol
- Plasma Rifle
- Needler

Dual Magnums

Using Dual Magnums is what char likes to call "John Woo-style fun". You have to be accurate with both Magnums for this to be effective. The guns are semi-automatic so you must have good aim and pull the triggers as fast as you can. Once the target's shields are down, the headshot bonus of two Magnums will make quick work of him.

This duo is especially popular in the Snipers game type. Of course, the Magnums are far more effective once your opponent's shields are down. However, if you are able to get in close, you could catch the sniper by surprise.

Bring it on!

Magnum + Plasma Pistol

This can be a lightning fast combination punch. Overload the Plasma Pistol and fire a ball at your target. Once his shields are down, use the Magnum's head shot bonus to finish. If this is done properly, there is very little that could save your opponent. The cons of using this technique are that you need to be in close for it to be effective and running around with an overcharged Plasma Pistol lights you up like a Christmas tree.

SMG + Plasma Pistol

This combination may not be as fast as the Plasma Pistol with the Magnum, but it does have its benefits. The idea is the same: knock out shields with a single plasma ball and then open up with the other hand. However, your SMG is a spray weapon. It may not be as fast as the Magnum but it requires less accuracy and it has a bigger clip.

Crew 116 Advice: SMG + Plasma Pistol

Once you can get the feel for holding down one trigger while tapping the other one (it is easier than it sounds), this is the best DW combo in the game.

—MrJukes

SMG + Plasma Rifle

Use the Plasma Rifle to take out your opponents' shields and then finish them off with the SMG. This combination allows you a little bit of room to work since both weapons spray at medium range. If, for instance, you are retreating from a Shotgun or a Plasma Sword, then this is a great combination to have in your mitts.

Crew 116 Advice: SMG and Plasma Rifle

This combination is great for up-close DW action. The Plasma Rifle sprays too much for my tastes over range. (Unless you pulse it, but you don't want to do that in a hectic fight where the opponent is paying attention.) Up close though, the plasma carves through the shields and the SMG does the rest.

—char

Dual Plasma Rifle

This is better than the SMG and Plasma Pistol up close but not as useful at range. The Plasma Rifle sprays more than the SMG so you'll really need to be right next to your target.

Crew 116 Advice: Dual Plasma Rifles

The only time I ever use Dual Plasma Rifles is on Midship because there are so many of them. Not a very powerful combination.

—MrJukes

Dual Needlers

This is a fun combination but only useful in certain situations, such as firing into the Lockout courtyard or an open space on Burial Mounds. Don't use dual Needlers unless you have room to get away and your target is exposed. If you get into a close fight with these, you'll probably go down before the needles you fired even explode.

This can be an effective combination if you're badly outnumbered. You may not survive the battle but the homing needle shards can find multiple targets to take with you. If you're on a Kamikaze infiltration into an open space, you might want to consider this combination. Run in with both Needlers blazing and you could pin cushion a bunch of surprised enemy defenders.

One of my favorite combos.

Dual SMG

The SMG can be found all over the place. For this reason alone, you will often see people using this combo. It works up close but not as fast as some of the aforementioned combinations. If someone gets your shields down, you probably don't want to stand your ground with these.

Practice Tip:

You should not only try out these dual weapon combos, you should also practice with each weapon so that you can get used to the effective range of everything in your arsenal.

Make use of the best possible combos.

Final Thoughts

Here are a few quick tips that don't easily fit into the other categories, but they are important to know. These types of tips are discovered over time so it simply isn't possible to list them all. Check Halo 2 fan sites and www.halobattleguide.com for more of this type of information.

Sword Combo Punch

This is a fun move. When you have the sword, try this sequence: trigger, melee, trigger. The effect is three hits with the Plasma Sword. It isn't as deadly as the lunge, but it's far more interesting. The first time someone did this to me, my jaw dropped and I immediately tried to figure out what had happened.

Spawn Melee

If you are caught in a lockdown situation, do a quick melee attack just as you spawn. This will move your head and may be just enough to throw off a spawn camper.

Practice Tip:

If you want to practice headshots, then create a game type that will favor accurate hits. For example, use 400% health and no shields. In this configuration, headshot bonuses will be fatal but body shots could take up to a full clip. This drill can also help you remember which weapons offer the headshot bonus.

Improving Your Play

The best way to become a better player is to swallow your pride and take a serious look at your game. You will not improve simply by playing often; you also need to consciously alter your game. Even advanced players have plenty of opportunities to improve their play. Here are a few keys to improving your play:

- **Play to win.** If you want to be a top-level player, you should use everything at your disposal to win. Refer to Chapter 10, Wort Wort Wort! Halo 2 Etiquette, if you feel apprehensive about using the techniques at your disposal. In addition, remember that practice doesn't make perfect—only perfect practice makes perfect. When you're playing, make the right decisions. Don't promote bad habits because you think that you will win.

- **Know your game.** Figure out what you do well and what skills you could improve. Be honest with yourself when you assess your game. If you can't drop opponents with a single Sniper Rifle shot, then don't convince yourself that you're a champion sniper.

- **Find players who are better than you are.** While it might be fun to dominate your buddies, playing against people above your skill level will bring up your game. Look for challenges, not empty victories.

- **Know your enemy.** Knowing your opponent's skills is almost as important as knowing your own game. I still remember when I found out about the orange fleshy part of a Hunter's lower back. That one piece of information completely changed the Halo 1 campaign dynamic. Instead of using rockets, I would use a single Pistol shot. Watch your opponents play and figure out their metaphorical 'orange flesh.' For example, if a player is an expert sniper, find out how good he is in a close fight. If someone consistently takes you down with the Plasma Sword, see how she likes the business end of the Battle Rifle.

- **Pay attention to what other players are doing.** If a player surprises you in some unusual way, try to figure out what happened. It may be a tactic that you could use.

- **Check Halo 2 web sites for updates on strategy and tips.** As gamers play Halo 2, they will come up with numerous tips and tricks. Stay up to date by checking online resources such as www.halobattleguide.com.

- **Play different game types.** If you want to be a great player, then don't just play the one game type that you enjoy the most. Mix in some variety; it will help you improve your game.

Find a weakness.

- **Play the single player campaign on the Legendary difficulty.** If you're going to practice, you may as well challenge yourself. If you find that Legendary is too tough, work your way up by playing the other settings first.

- **Get comfortable with all the Halo 2 weapons.** You may not like them all, but you should be fearsome with each.

Practice Tip:

Any game that focuses on one weapon is a great drill. Spending an entire game with a single weapon helps you learn when the weapon is powerful and when it is weak. For example, after playing a whole game with the Shotgun, you start to get a good understanding of its effective range.

Chapter 6: Solo Strategy

Solo strategy is obviously crucial when it comes to Free For All (FFA) games. However, it is equally important when you are playing with your clan. There is a wide gap between the team's strategy and a single player's ability to contribute to that plan. Therefore, each player must have the personal skills to help the team realize its goal.

Whereas the Advanced Combat chapter equipped you with specific skills, this chapter is all about planning and decision making. Most Halo 2 games move quickly so you'll have to learn to make split second decisions based upon an ever changing environment.

In his Crew 116 profile, tantrum listed 'thinking' as his greatest strength. I believe that tantrum is a better player because he considers strategy to be a crucial element of his game. When given a choice between two players with comparable fighting skills, you will want the best strategist on your team.

The SPARTAN player model.

The Elite player model.

Have a Plan

Always have a clear and realistic objective. If you aren't sure what you are trying to do, you are playing without a plan and there is no way to determine whether you have succeeded or failed.

If you're averaging 20 deaths in your FFA matches, don't set your objective to be zero deaths. You certainly should push yourself to improve your performance, but it won't do you any good to choose an objective that isn't attainable or measurable.

Be specific. Don't just set out to win the game; break down how you will achieve that ultimate goal by considering which weapons and positions will work best for you on the current map. For example, your first objective may be to police the best weapon or to secure the best position.

Regardless of whether you are playing a team game or FFA, you should have an objective and a personal plan to achieve that objective when you start each game or each round.

Continually analyze your strategic choices. Let's say that you start an FFA game on Ivory Tower. You spawn in the basement and decide that your goal is to collect the Rocket Launcher. However, by the time you get to the SPANKr waterfall location, you find that the launcher is already gone and now you're out in the open. Since this puts you in a bad position, you are likely to consider this plan a failure. The next time you spawn in that location, you can try a different plan—such as collecting the Sword and hunting through the hallways. Analyzing your strategic choices will help you to determine exactly what style of play works best for you.

Unpredictability

Keep your opponents off balance by being creative. Just as erratic movements are the best way to dodge fire, unpredictable play is a vital strategy. If you develop a reputation, make sure it's for being a good player, not for always trying the same moves. Make a conscious effort to avoid falling into the following predictable patterns.

Going for the Same Weapon at the Same Time

One of my favorite defensive moves on the Ivory Tower map is to run up to the Overshield and then continue to the top of the tower. I can often get a free frag simply because so many people run straight for the Beam Rifle and immediately try to snipe.

I remember one game in particular when I was using this counterattack. The first round went well. As is often the case, the sniper was not paying attention and I was able to score a melee to the back of his head. The next round was a different story. When I came around the corner, there was a grenade coming right at me. In short, the sniper was a quick learner. Instead of putting him off balance, he turned the tables on me. However, if I had tried something different in the second round, he probably still would have thrown that grenade and he would have wasted time waiting for me to arrive.

Using the Same Route Around the Map

This is a bit of a gray area. There are times when you can produce excellent results by staying on a course that you know by heart. However, if you're playing against the same people a lot, they will also become familiar with your route. Mix it up a bit so that people don't camp on your path and

ambush you. Even switching direction can be an effective change.

Camping in the Same Place

I don't advocate camping, but if you are going to be a camper, don't be a dead camper. Choose different places to set up ambushes. If you don't adapt, your opponents will.

This also applies to defense fighting positions. For more about primary fighting positions, read Chapter 7, Team Strategy.

Practice Your Aim

When it comes to Halo 2 battles, the victor will usually be the player with the best weapon and aim—not the player who dodges the best. When analyzing your play, you should first look at ways that you can improve your offense and then worry about defensive moves that make you harder to hit. Most likely, you will see greater benefits working on your aim and weapon selection than you will by improving your dodging and evading skills.

The two caveats to this mindset are that you must master basic evasion and that you should be careful about which battles to enter in the first place. You can make yourself a harder target simply by 'short strafing' and being conscientious about when to engage.

> ### Crew 116 Advice: Hard Target or Hardcore Assassin?
>
> It's much easier to be a quick killer than it is to be hard to kill.
>
> —char

Fluidity

Fluidity in war is all about adaptation. You must learn to recognize factors that influence a battle and immediately react to them. For example, you might be engaged in a one-on-one fight against an FFA opponent. Imagine that as you are having a showdown a third player comes from behind both of you and fires an overcharged Plasma Pistol. You must instantly react to this change in the dynamic of the battle and decide whether you are going to stand your ground against these two players or retreat. What you should do depends on the situation and your ability to remain fluid in your game play.

> The way that is the way,
>
> Is not the eternal way.
>
> —Lao Tzu, *Tao Te Ching*

If you are struck by the Plasma Ball, you no longer have any shields and you now have two attackers facing you. In this case, I would retreat as fast as possible—although it's tough with no shield. I would not expect to win when I was wounded and outnumbered.

On the other hand, if your original combatant is injured, you now have the upper hand in the original battle. However, you also must now consider the third player. In this scenario, I would choose to charge the wounded player. By moving between the new attacker and the shield-less player, I reduce the chance that the new attacker will get the kill. If I am able to get through the wounded player, I would then egress in her direction as I short-hopped a grenade and attempted to fend off the new player.

> **Note:**
>
> Of course, after you've survived the battle, you should analyze whether you could have avoided a bad situation such as this near double-team example.

Fluidity also includes the ability to adapt quickly enough to maintain the initiative, which is covered in detail later in this chapter. In team games, fluidity is largely dependent upon your ability to maintain communication with your team. However, as a solo player fluidity is all about your decisions. Don't expect to always make the right call but learn from your mistakes and correct them.

> Each episode of war is the temporary result of a unique combination of circumstance... creating a continuous, fluctuating fabric replete with fleeting opportunities and unforeseen events.
>
> —*Warfighting, The U.S. Marine Corps Book of Strategy*

Take advantage of chaos.

The most common FFA test of your flexibility is your ability to engage multiple targets. Remember that most of the time, FFA players don't care who they go after because they are concerned with frags, not people. When you find you're engaging multiple targets, use the gambit from the old *Mission Impossible* TV show and get them to fight each other. That way you can sit back and clean up the mess. Pulling this off might be as simple as ducking behind cover long enough for the rest of the crowd to turn their reticle onto another player.

Distraction and misdirection are your friends as they both affect your opponents' ability to remain fluid. By making the enemy think you're doing something other than what you really intend to do, you can take advantage of the enemy's confusion.

Crew 116 Advice: Fluidity

You have to adapt to the game quickly. It's not about camping, but figuring out what is right for that moment.

For example, let's say that I'm running along the center path in Waterworks and I see a Ghost coming at me. What's my best move? Ideally, I can make it to the ladders in the center without getting run over and climb up. Then I get a weapon and cover from the Ghost. If I can't make it, perhaps I can jump up on the lip of the path and avoid being rammed that way. Maybe the best thing to do is retreat.

Fluidity is a constant analysis of what options you have and what your opponent is doing.

—*char*

Assessing the Battlefield

The battlefield is your arena. You should strive to learn all about the conditions of your fight. In MSG Brett A. Stoneberger's popular handbook of basic combat skills, *Combat Leader's Field Guide* (Stackpole Books), he identifies the following key battlefield elements:

- Objective
- Maneuvers
- Firepower
- Surprise
- Initiative

Note:

Combat Leader's Field Guide (Stackpole Books) is an essential read for soldiers and other security forces operating in combat units, so MSG Stoneberger's insights will be incredibly valuable to you in developing your own combat strategies.

Objective

You should have a goal in mind each time you engage in battle. The objective must be specific, measurable, and realistic. In team games, the overall objective can be easily defined—for example, to plant a bomb in the other team's base. In addition, team members have their own personal objectives related to their team role. Team members' personal objectives are similar to objectives in a solo game.

Maneuvers

A great deal of modern military strategy focuses on the principles of maneuverability. As a single soldier, you can gain the upper hand in many battles by shifting your position. For example, something as simple as strafing behind a corner could be enough to throw off an attacker. While the other player fires into a wall, you can reload or preserve your ammo for a counterattack.

Examples of strategic movements include flanking attacks and defensive flank positioning. However, this is just the tip of the iceberg when it comes to maneuvers. When you have a squad to work with, movement becomes even more important. Chapter 7, Team Strategy, covers the concept of maneuvering in detail.

An exposed flank.

Firepower

In military terms, firepower is more than just the weaponry in your arsenal; it is also a measure of your ability to bring that firepower to bear on your target. This is yet another reminder that you should use the right weapon for the right job. For example, you wouldn't want to have a Rocket Launcher in your hands while fighting in a narrow corridor—chances are that you'll take a suicide.

In Halo 2, weapon superiority is a key factor in every battle. You should make an effort to outgun your adversaries, especially when you are on your own. This is not only useful for winning fights, but also for winning quickly.

You want to drop players as fast as possible so that you avoid getting an 'add.' This expression refers to the common FFA circumstance where you're in a fight and someone comes in to attempt to take frags for both you and your combatant. In addition, the faster the battle ends, the less damage to your shields.

Surprise

Of all military elements, surprise is probably the most exciting. A well-planned ambush or sneaky maneuver can certainly turn the tide of any battle.

When you examine your game play, look for opportunities to use surprise. Generally, this is easier if you know the territory inside and out. If you do not, you're more likely to be the victim of a surprise maneuver. Find ways to move around the map that give you the chance to surprise other players. The element of surprise determines the outcome of many battles.

Initiative

In modern warfare, initiative is of paramount importance. The force that has the initiative controls the battlefield by determining where and when important events happen. As a singleton, your goal is to maintain the initiative by yourself. Whether you are in an offensive or defensive stance, you should know what you want to do.

Large FFA games are chaotic but that certainly doesn't mean that you're powerless to influence the outcome of the game. An expert player will use tactics such as weapon superiority and flanking to maintain the initiative.

Remember that you don't have to be attacking to have the initiative. If you have set up an ambush, then you have the initiative. You are most powerful when you know that you have the advantage but your enemy believes that he has the initiative. This situation will cause your enemy to engage at the wrong time—a mistake that you can exploit.

Determining When to Engage

The most important strategy decision for each player is when to engage in battle. Once you have engaged the enemy, you will be in either an offensive posture or a defensive posture. You may decide to switch quickly from one posture to the other, but your current posture will determine how you behave in combat. For example, if your shields are down, you will be defensive and dodge fire. However, if you are strong, you may choose to charge.

The following sections examine your key considerations when determining whether you should engage.

Can I Win This Fight?

Most of the time, you only want to engage when you believe that you can win the fight; however, winning isn't the only objective. There are times when other considerations warrant a sacrifice. Quite often, you will have the option to bug out of a fight if necessary. The ability to assess whether you can win is a skill that you will learn through experience.

Consider the following factors as they relate to both you and your opponent when deciding whether to engage:

- Cover
- Position
- Weapons in possession
- Shield status
- Clip status
- Retreat options
- Potential for team backup
- Relative skill levels
- Element of surprise

Natural players probably consider all of these factors without ever being conscious of having made a decision. If it doesn't come naturally to you, don't despair. With practice and thoughtful evaluation, you will develop the ability to assess these factors as a split second reflex.

Keep in mind that one of the easiest feints to make is hiding a powerful weapon and then switching when the opponent engages. If someone comes at you with a single Magnum, you should wonder what she is hiding.

In a Halo 2 game, you must exploit the factors under your control that affect your ability to win a fight. Try to shift all of these factors in your favor and then you will be free to engage more often.

For example, you should consciously do things such as:

- Use cover when you fight.
- Avoid being cornered.
- Fight when your shields are up.
- Use the best weapon possible for the fight.
- Learn to count shots and reload when it's safe to do so.
- When playing team games, tell your team that you're going in so that they can help.

Is This an Important Target?

Another key consideration that affects your decision to engage is whether the fight is worth the effort and time. The topic of prioritizing your targets is discussed later in this chapter.

Crew 116 Advice: Counting Shots

Count your enemies' shots. Rockets, sniper rounds, and grenades are easy. When you can count their Battle Rifle or Carbine fire, you're golden.

—*char*

Time to retreat.

Will This Fight Help My Team Even if I Lose?

It may seem strange, but in some game types, collecting frags doesn't mean anything and dying can be irrelevant. In these games, strategically picking targets is about the overall goal rather than your own ability to win the fight. There are cases when tagging someone could enable him to re-spawn in a better position to defend his base. If you know that your team is mounting an assault, you don't want to send reinforcements.

In these games, pick confrontations that will benefit the current situation. If you find someone on his own and he isn't in a position to make an assault, then you might want to let him be. Tagging him will take ammunition, give away your position, and it could make your overall position worse.

Similarly, you shouldn't worry about dying if your sacrifice will serve the ultimate goal of the game. This could mean that you throw yourself into FFA fights because you only need one more frag, or you pick up a flag so that it doesn't return to the base. As tantrum from Crew 116 advises, "throwing [yourself] at the problem" can pay off. For example, in a lockdown it may take several attempts to get by the other team. However, once you are through, they will have to break their focus on the lockdown.

An Elite throwing his body at the problem.

Finding Targets

Finding targets is especially important when you are playing an FFA match. The game is a race so you need to locate targets quickly. Use the following techniques when you are hunting.

Use a Circuit Around the Map

Although you don't want to be predictable in your movement, using a path for tracking can be helpful. There are certain vulnerable positions on the map, so you should find a route that allows you to check these positions while maintaining your security.

Keep in mind that the high traffic areas are often the most vulnerable and the most valuable. For example, the Lockout courtyard offers no cover but it's also a great place to pick up targets. Find ways to catch others in the open while maintaining your own security.

Noises and Voices

Most noises in a Halo 2 game are an indication of battle. As mentioned in Chapter 5, Advanced Combat, make sure that you're making the most of all of your senses. If you don't have a great stereo, you might want to try headphones. This may help you figure out the direction of a sound. Once you use noise to find a fight you can 'add' to the battle and try to take advantage of the weakened players.

Similarly, the proximity vocals of other players could tip you off that someone is nearby. If you don't want others to find you this way, either mute your mike or make sure that you're quiet. Personally, I have difficulty not reacting to the game so the mute button is my friend.

The Reticle

If you believe that someone is lurking in the shadows, remember that your reticle will turn red when it is over a player. In addition, the Covenant Needler shards have limited tracking abilities. Another option is to fire off a few needles and see if they lock on to anyone.

Found you!

HUD Markers

In team games, you have the benefit of using the team markers. The most obvious use for this indicator is that it is one way to see which players are on your team. This can be useful in a dark area where you don't have time to figure out the color of the player in front of you. However, the markers tell you a lot more about your teammates.

There are three colors for the team indicators:

- White—healthy teammate
- Yellow—teammate taking fire
- Red—recently deceased teammate

Although dead teammates could mean trouble, it may also indicate the location of an opponent weakened from battle with your teammates. If you are playing a Slayer game, you might want to try to engage the victor of the battle.

Prioritize Your Targets

There are many times when you must select which target to fight. The best choice depends on the type of game that you are playing.

If you are playing an FFA game, then the answer is straightforward. FFA is a race and for that reason you want to be in almost any fight that you think you can win. One previously mentioned exception to this is if you have the Active Camouflage. If you're invisible, you may choose to forego some fights in order to cover more ground, take a position, grab a weapon, or hunt a specific target.

When it comes to team games, you have to consider whether the target at hand is the best use of your time. As the number of players increases, it becomes imperative to focus on the important battles.

If you're playing offense in a team game, you don't want to fight every opponent on the way to the opponent's base. While you are moving toward your objective, you're more interested in getting there than engaging the enemy. If you choose to fight every player in your way, you will likely see them again when you reach their base. Also, if you are constantly engaging the enemy, the defensive squad will know that you're coming. Giving notice may work in action movies, but generally you should try not to announce your presence before it's necessary.

On the other hand, if you're playing defense in a team game, you will have to engage almost all attackers that come your way. Unless you're setting up an ambush, you want to slow down anyone that comes toward your position.

Choose wisely.

Key considerations when you are prioritizing your enemy are:

Is the Player an Immediate Threat to You?

If you believe that you're in personal jeopardy, then you may choose to concentrate on the player who is attacking you.

Is the Enemy an Immediate Threat to Your Goals?

If you are playing an FFA match and you know that someone has a big lead, you may choose to go after that specific player. In a team game, you will want to choose the player that is threatening your team. In other words, the guy across the map may be in the open but he isn't your best target if someone else is running right at the Rocket Launcher.

Furthermore, a player running with the flag will often be more important to you than someone who is trying to take you out. When you are playing team defense, analyzing the biggest threat to the team is the best way to pick your fights.

How Good Is the Target?

If you know your enemy, you might want to go after the best players first. This will free you up to fight other battles with greater ease. On the other hand, if you know that someone is far above your skill level, you may choose to go for weaker targets and avoid conflict. This could work in a Slayer game, but in team games, you probably won't have this luxury.

What Weapon Is the Opponent Holding?

Normally, if you run into someone with the Rocket Launcher, your best bet is to bug out and find another victim. However, if you're sniping, the guy with the Rocket Launcher might be your best target. If you are playing a team game, then you'll certainly be doing your team a favor.

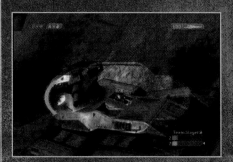

I choose this guy.

How Healthy Is the Guy in Your Reticle?

If you know that a player is injured, then you should exploit your advantage over that player. You should take down the wounded player just because it offers a quick victory. If you are healthy and your target is running without shields, you certainly have the odds in your favor.

Are You Out for Revenge?

Psychological warfare can influence a Halo 2 game. My advice is to take the high ground. Don't compromise your strategy for the sake of revenge. However, there are times when you should encourage your opponents to do so. If you can convince your opponent to play for revenge, he may not be thinking clearly about his objectives.

Flanking

When attacking, you want to maneuver into the most powerful position. This often includes exposing a weak side of your enemy, which is known as flanking your target. In Halo 2, the weakest side of any player is the player's back. If you are able to move stealthily around to a player's back, you will most often win the fight.

The next four images show how a quick flanking move can be crucial during a heated FFA battle. In this example, three players meet and engage in a chaotic showdown. At the beginning of the battle, player A is in a dual with player B when player C comes around the corner and enters the fight. Player A is in an exposed position so she decides to

flank player C. Player A retreats and takes cover, forcing player B to adjust her focus to deal with the new threat of player C. Player C chooses to engage the immediate threat presented by player B, taking his focus off of player A. While the other two players fight it out, player A is recharging his shields. Player A determines that his best option for survival is to assume that player C will defeat player B, who is weak from fighting. When player C defeats player B, player A can take advantage of his cover to flank player C.

The next set of figures show the position of the three players after the flanking move. Player C defeats player B and player A has successfully flanked player C. Since player C has been wounded, it is likely that player A will be the last one standing.

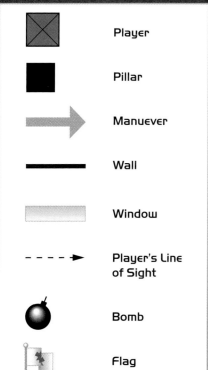

Maneuvers legend.

	Player
	Pillar
	Manuever
	Wall
	Window
	Player's Line of Sight
	Bomb
	Flag

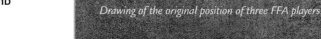

Drawing of the original position of three FFA players.

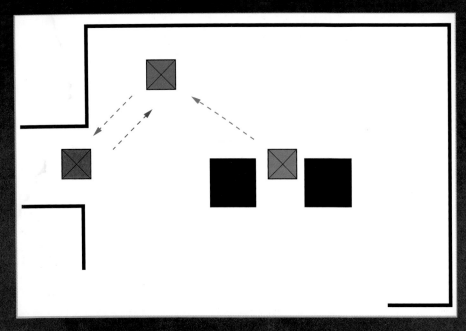

Drawing of the position after the flanking maneuver.

Original position of three FFA players.

Position after player A performs a flanking maneuver.

Feinting

Generally speaking, most Halo players do not try to deceive one another. However, these players are not taking advantage of all the resources that they have at their disposal. Deception should be a weapon that you're comfortable using when the opportunity presents itself.

> "Warfare is one thing.
> It is a philosophy of deception.
> When you are ready, you try to appear incapacitated.
> When active, you pretend inactivity.
> When you are close to the enemy, you appear distant.
> When far away, you pretend you are near."
>
> —Sun Tzu, *The Art of War*

The most common military deception is the feint. Your goal is to make your adversary believe something that isn't true. The example of someone hiding a powerful weapon is a classic way to make a feint. The deceptive player attracts attention with a weak weapon and thereby tricks his target into believing that he is vulnerable. The opponent then makes the decision to engage a player who actually has the initiative. Once he sees that his feinting was successful, the deceiving player pulls out a stronger weapon to fight.

Just like a poker player, you might eventually get a reputation for your deadly bluffs. If that happens, you can make the most of people's reluctance to attack you. When you are actually carrying nothing but an SMG, your opponent might think twice about following you around a corner.

A smart Halo 2 player will figure out innovative ways to trick opponents. Remember that the tension of a chaotic encounter will only emphasize the advantage you get from making a successful feint.

Crew 116 Advice: Voice Feints

Voice works great in team games. For example, someone yells, "Hey, flag guy, don't run out the back door!" When in reality, they're going out the front, but the defenders all run to the back. We pulled this off a couple of times.

—*char*

Crew 116 Advice: Feinting

I'll often try to lure people in close by pretending that I don't see them. Once they're in close, I finish them off.

—*char*

In Halo 2, a great way to do this would be to spray someone with a single machine gun and then retreat around a corner. When the sucker rounds the corner, there you are waiting with a Plasma Sword. Some people refer to this type of maneuver as 'playing possum.'

Oops, I thought you had an SMG...

Playing the High Ground

Controlling the high ground is a traditional battlefield advantage. As a Halo 2 gamer, one must respect this tradition. Playing the high ground gives you a better view of the battlefield, it gives you bigger targets to shoot at, and it often means that your attackers have to use well-known routes to get to your position.

Even in the virtual world of Halo 2, 'gravity' is an important consideration. Fragmentation Grenades are often easier to throw downhill than uphill. With Plasma Grenades, you generally won't be trying to bounce them, but you can see more of your opponent when looking down. This gives you a larger target. Unless you are aiming for an enclosed area, you can drop both types of grenades with more precision when aiming downhill.

Some people feel that aiming up gives you a clear shot at an opponent's head and therefore there isn't much of an advantage when looking down. This isn't quite true; you may be able to see a player's head, but that's all that you can see. When looking down, you can usually see the player's head and at least part of his body. Remember that aiming at the body is a good idea when your target has his shields up.

In addition, being above your opponents gives you the option of 'dropping in.' When you jump down on someone, you'll usually get a free hit before he even realizes that you are there.

The lower sniper perch on the Lockout level is a great example of how playing the high ground can give you an advantage. First, you run to the top and grab the rifle, then you go back down to the platform that gives you a clear view over the entire courtyard plus the approaches. When you perform this maneuver, you have the Sniper Rifle and your opponents do not (unless someone got it before you took your position). Secondly, the two common approaches are clearly visible. The courtyard approach requires a jump toward the business end of your rifle, and the ramp approach reveals the attacker on your motion tracker. In addition, for anyone to get above you, he would first have to get by you. However, the real beauty of being in this location is that you can drop in on the ramp approach. When you see someone coming from below, simply watch over the edge as he starts up the ramp. At this point, jump down behind him and smite him with a melee to the neck.

Of course, there is a less common approach to this perch that you cannot cover. Someone coming across the courtyard can crouch jump up to the sniper tower without your knowledge. After all, what fun would an invincible location be to anyone? (For details of the multiplayer maps, see Chapter 8, Multiplayer Maps.)

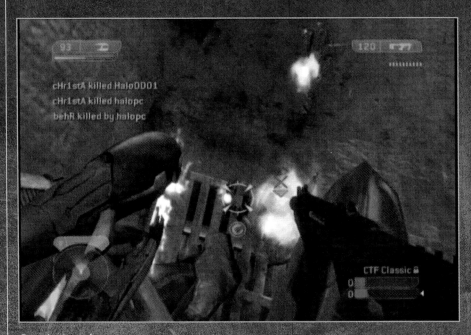

Dropping in on the party.

A good strategy and a nice view.

Using the Environment

Expert players are acutely aware of their surroundings. They know that any slight advantage will pay off when they encounter another skilled gamer. With this in mind, you should not only learn where weapons are, you should also study all of the maps for environmental advantages.

A prime example of this is discarded Covenant fusion cores. I can still remember trying to convince a buddy that he should pay attention to them. I convinced him to target one with the Sniper Rifle just to try it out. Much to my amusement, there happened to be someone hiding nearby. It was a complete fluke, but it was his first Halo 2 frag so he's now a believer. Whenever he gets the chance, he'll check for fodder hanging out by an unexploded core.

Also, note that you may want to set off a core as a defensive tactic. If you need to stand near the site of one of these powder kegs, you should probably explode it before someone else uses it on you.

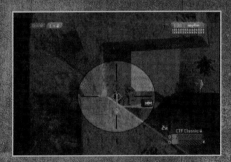

Targeting Covenant fusion cores.

Other environmental considerations include anything that can be moved, activated, or destroyed. For example, when you attack the Zanzibar base, it's in your best interest to open the main gate. This increases the options for your team.

Crew 116 Advice: Gate Feint

You can make some good feints using the Zanzibar gate entrance. After opening the gate, drive a jeep to the open door and run the flag out the front.

—char

Opening the Zanzibar gate is a good idea.

Messing with the Enemy

Technically, these techniques are known as *psychological warfare*. However, I like the sound of *messing with the enemy* better. Essentially, your goal is to confuse or anger the enemy. This section explores some of the easiest ways to irritate your opposition.

In order to throw someone off his game, you may choose to toss these techniques into the mix. Just keep in mind that some people will actually play better when they are enraged.

Trash Talk

Talking trash is certainly a tradition that dates back long before FPS games. While most people will use it simply to aggravate other players, a few actually use trash talk as part of their strategy. For example, saying something like, "I'm gonna smack you with a rocket," could convince the other player that you will be heading toward the Rocket Launcher. However, your actual plan may be to ambush a choke point on the way to the launcher. When the other player tries to get to where he believes you are located, you have created a degree of surprise just by using trash talk.

Melee Attack

No one enjoys being put down by a forearm. It's just plain embarrassing, especially for a good player. Just remember that you had better have a strong short-range weapon if your mark turns at the wrong time. Don't get yourself fragged because of your lust for the smack down.

Sticky Grenades

Next to the melee death, being stuck with a Plasma Grenade is probably the worst way to go. There is a certain helplessness in this attack that will get under the skin of the most stoic player. To add insult to injury, the status message will show that you were stuck.

Oh, she's not going to like that.

Single Sniper Shot

Even if it has nothing to do with his assignment, a player will proudly cross the entire map to hunt a sniper that just tagged him. Generally, it isn't the midfield sniper that annoys people—after all, he's just doing his job. The aggravating sniper is the guy exploiting that spot that everyone knows is a camper's dream. No matter how cheap you think he is, don't let that guy distract you from your goal.

'Hitting' a Corpse

Yes, it's true, whacking a corpse can enrage your victim. However, there are other things that you can do to a body that will send someone's blood boiling. You'll just have to figure this one out for yourself.

Getting Around

Easily making your way around a level is vital to any FPS game. However, people fail to realize that using non-conventional ways to get around is also important.

To compete as a top Halo 2 gamer, you must know all the ways to get from one place to another. Furthermore, whenever it is appropriate, one must use these tricky ways to move around the map.

Some of the unconventional ways to move include using walls or other objects to climb, rocket jumping, grenade jumping, and crouching while you jump. Crouching during a jump can help you make longer jumps because your feet won't get caught as quickly. When you explore levels, you should be looking for opportunities to use these techniques. (For more information about trick jumps, see Chapter 8, Multiplayer Maps.)

Of course, you also have to consider the standard ways to move quickly around the map. These include vehicles, elevators, and transporters. Learn where the vehicles spawn, where the transporters take you, and when it is best to use elevators.

One problem with elevators and transporters is that they tend to attract campers. Make sure that you are on your guard when you use them.

An unconventional path.

Running Weapons

When you come across a powerful weapon that you do not wish to use, you may decide to hide it from your enemy. One way to accomplish this is to blast it around with explosions. However, there is another option that won't cost you any ammunition. Simply run up to the weapon and use the 'X' button to pick it up; this will throw your current weapon forward a bit. If you continue running, you will be over the weapon that you just dropped. By running forward and picking up the weapon that you just dropped, you can move the weapon around the map. All you have to do is switch a few times and you'll probably be able to find a nice dark area to hide the weapon that you chose not to carry. Once you have hidden the weapon, you can notify your teammates so they will know where to look for it. Just keep in mind that the game will eventually re-spawn the weapon back in its original location.

One thing to keep in mind when you are running weapons is that objects occasionally disappear in the Halo universe. For example, if a wall or a large pile of other weapons is nearby, I wouldn't recommend dropping something in the area. You could find that the one weapon that you needed just disappeared into the pile or dropped into a crack in the floor.

Example Game Types

It is important not only to be familiar with each of the built-in Halo 2 game types, but also to understand the differences in them. Remember that you can create your own variations of the provided games.

Crew 116 Advice: FFA Game Type

DW early and often. When you spawn, grab a second gun until you can upgrade. Grenades are weaker than in Halo 1, and up close, few things beat DW. Take advantage of others; if two people are fighting, sweep in and kill them both. After a successful fight, take a second to get your shields back before charging back into battle. Know the map and when weapons spawn. Remember that weapon superiority is key.

—*char*

Slayer

Most people don't think of FFA games as a race, but they are. You are trying to get to a point total before your opponents. This generally means that you must be in the action constantly. Of course, you must balance this fact with the reality that you can only score while you are alive. Essentially, you want to pick the right battles, but be aggressive.

In FFA games, the significance of dying decreases with the number of people in the game. For example, in a 16-player game, if you get dropped once by each player, you are still only one point back. Even though you died 15 times, all you need is one frag to catch up. So in FFA you can take just about every gamble to get an extra frag. If it works out once in four tries in a four-person game, then you're breaking even. Never back down in a big FFA game, and play very aggressively even if it's just a four-person game.

In Team Slayer games, smaller teams sometimes have an advantage because they have more targets to shoot. If you are outnumbering the other team, make sure you work together to eliminate any chance that the opponents get an advantage.

Slayer Variants

Elimination: In this game, you only get one life. Your goal is to be the last player standing. Some people will frantically avoid battle until the field is significantly smaller.

Phantoms: All players are invisible but your teammates have navigation indicators so you know how far away they are from you.

Rockets: All players start with Rocket Launchers and there are plenty of rockets on the map. People call this a *twitch game* because you need to react quickly.

Snipers: All players start with a Sniper Rifle. Make sure that you move around; don't give anyone an easy shot at you. You may want to stay near a Magnum pistol so that you can quickly dual wield if someone decides to try a John Woo style showdown.

Rockets will test your reflexes.

They shouldn't be doing that in the open.

Probably the most tense you will feel playing Halo 2.

Swords: In this new game, all players start with the impressive Plasma Sword. When you first play the swords game type, it can be spooky. There is a sublime silence that comes with a game that lacks constant gunshot or explosion noises. If you like using the sword, you'll dig this game.

Crew 116 Advice: Snipers

This game type is similar to FFA. If your opponent is a great sniper, fight him up close. If he's good up close, tag him from range. Both skills should be honed for you to be successful in this game type.

Make sure that you keep moving. If you take a sniper shot, the trail is obvious. Also, people tend to stay in one place, so moving around the map will help you find them. Avoid open, exposed areas.

—char

Crew 116 Advice: Swords

You can dodge the sword lunge. To do this you need to cut to the side right when you think the opponent will lunge. Be careful not to lunge off ledges or at obstacles that will stop the lunge. The melee attack on the sword is better up close than the lunge.

—char

Assault

In standard Assault, each team gets two rounds to plant the bomb. In Neutral Assault, there is only one bomb and both teams are trying to plant it at the enemy base.

Tick...tick...tick...

Crew 116 Advice: Assault

Similar to CTF, except you're down a man while carrying the bomb. Don't be afraid to drop the bomb and fight. Don't worry about the indicator so much; it's obvious where it's going.

—*char*

Capture the Flag

Capture the Flag is the most popular team game. The goal is to steal the other team's flag and return it to your base for the capture. In One Flag CTF, there are rounds and each team gets a chance to play offense and defense. Remember that flag captures do not influence your Halo 2 ranking. Your rank in the carnage report means nothing; you will only win if your team wins.

CTF is a fan favorite.

Crew 116 Advice: Capture the Flag

Obviously, FFA skills still apply here. If you don't win fights, you won't get to the flag. On offense, attack as a team. Single flag hopper games have short timers for each round, and you basically get one good push. Set up the attack from multiple sides and push at the same time. If you botch it, set up again quickly.

If you are carrying the flag and going to die, toss it somewhere useful. Don't leave it in the middle of an open field where it's trivial to defend. It might make sense to throw it behind you if it's a hard to cover area. Often caps go sour because someone dies and leaves the flag in a rough spot.

Vehicles can be effective. A flag leaving in a jeep is nearly unstoppable. Make sure you have a strong offense to support the vehicles, because you're effectively down a man for every driver.

On defense, hold the midfield and watch for people trying to sneak around. A solo player in the base isn't terrible, but letting their whole team get there is bad.

If everyone is dead and the flag is getting away, don't chase it if it's too far ahead. Head for the other team's cap point and try to defend it. The flag is slow and often people don't take an optimal route (usually because they're avoiding fire). If you have access to a vehicle, you're probably better off to grab a ride and blitz for the other team's base. Usually Ghosts are the best choice for this.

—*char*

King of the Hill

King of the Hill (KotH) is a great game. The object of the game is to accumulate time by standing within a certain designated 'hill' position on the map. The hill is marked with a navigation indicator and the game ends when a player or team has accumulated the necessary time.

Crew 116 Advice: King of the Hill

This is a lockdown game type. Try to get weapons and position, and then take the hill back. Once you control the hill, put the weakest offensive player in the hill and have the rest fan out to stop the opponent's advance. Go far enough out that if you die, you'll have time to re-spawn in the hill and move out again.

Remember that you get time even if the opponent is in the hill. If you are fighting around the hill, try to stay in it to get time. Sitting in the hill with invis can get you free time.

—char

A player trying to stand her ground at the hill.

King of the Hill Variants

Team King: This is a team version of KotH.

Crazy King: Just like in Halo 1, Crazy King is King of the Hill with a moving hill location.

Crew 116 Advice: Crazy King

Stay near the border not right at the hill. (Use the) same strategy as above, except you want to be able to be more mobile. Once the hill moves, head to the next one and set up shop. If the opponents beat you there, make sure they don't keep re-spawning in the hill; kill them quickly.

—char

Territories

This is a new game type. The idea is to accumulate time by occupying as many territories as possible. The more territories that you own, the faster you accrue time. (Read more about this game type in Chapter 7, Team Strategy.)

The new Territory game type adds an interesting element to the mix.

Oddball

The goal of this game is to carry the ball for two minutes. Your opponents will try to take the ball away from you. Use the 'Back' button to see how much time players have accumulated.

Some people like to hide with the ball by using elevators or transporters. When an opponent approaches, the player with the ball takes the elevator or moves through the transporter. This makes it harder for the other players to find him. Some people consider this technique to be poor manners. (For more examples of contentious behavior, refer to Chapter 10, Wort Wort Wort! Halo 2 Etiquette.)

The Halo® 2 Oddball.

Crew 116 Advice: Oddball

Similar to KotH, but you can be mobile. Take the ball where you can defend it.

—*char*

Juggernaut

It is back with some new variants. The Juggernaut does more damage with weapons. To steal his powers, you must beat the Juggernaut. You need to score 10 kills to win.

You want to be the Juggernaut.

Crew 116 Advice: Ninjanaut

One game type we'll probably see more of is 'Ninjanaut' (in which) the Juggernaut is invisible and has infinite ammo.

—*char*

Chapter 7: Team Strategy

If you're a fan of strategic action games, then Halo 2 team games are right for you. While FFA games are primarily decided by the skills of one player, team games require that players perform well as part of a group effort. This chapter explores the topic of strategy in the team arena.

In the Halo 1 'attract mode' demos, there are a few scenes where two people are playing cooperatively. For example, there is one scene where two players drive up to a structure in a Warthog. The gunner lays down suppressing fire through one opening, while the driver hops out and goes around the side. The Covenant troops are fully occupied with the Warthog chain gun so there are some easy kills for the flanking player; of course, he would have done better if he had reloaded before he got in the jeep. Nonetheless, this short demo is a good example of how a smart team can overwhelm an opposing force.

While it is possible to use these maneuvers in isolation, they become far more effective when combined. Your team will be able to exploit the weaknesses of your opponents by stringing together a number of maneuvers. Some of these strategies may sound far-out but they can often be combined to great effect.

Team games can be the most dramatic.

Fundamentals of Team Play

The team must have a plan.

An organized team always has an advantage over an ad hoc team. By laying out a clear plan, you can best allocate the resources available to you.

Everyone on the team must have an assigned role.

Having a clear plan must include a specific role for each member of the team. This is one of the factors that allows Crew 116 to perform so well. Not only is their team organized, but they also have a role for each team member.

Everyone must know what is happening at all times.

Talk it up. It's that simple. You must communicate with your teammates so that everyone has a chance to react to quickly changing circumstances. Remember that the "fog of war" is famous for deciding the outcome of battles. Don't fall victim to the confusion created by poor communication.

Everyone must be able to quickly communicate any spot on any map.

This is one of the most important things that Crew 116 taught me. When it comes to map positions, it is imperative that your team has a common vocabulary. If you are serious about being a strong team, you should consider creating maps that show your team's names for every position on the level.

Planning for Battle

While you do not want to become inflexible, you also don't want to compromise your success because you didn't do your homework. The best defense against chaos is planning. These are some of the questions that you should ask yourself before you begin a campaign with your team.

What do you know about your team?

It is tough to wage a war when you don't know what resources you have at your disposal. Get to know the strengths and weaknesses of your team and compare these to the strengths and weaknesses of your opponents. Specific players will perform better in certain roles and probably even with specific weapons. Make sure that you know whether you are maximizing the potential of your squad.

Of course, some times you will be playing just for fun. If that's the case then you might switch people around to give them some variety. However, make sure that you know that you are doing this. If you really want to win, you should be playing to win.

The factors that add to battlefield chaos are referred to as 'friction.' Getting to know your team can help reduce battlefield friction. For example, some players will assume crucial tasks in particular maneuvers. Generally speaking, you will want to assign the best player possible to these tasks. If one of your crucial players fails his task, then you can immediately recognize that this is a significant threat to your team. If you don't know your team, you won't be able to gauge success or failure as quickly.

What do you know about the other team?

'Know your enemy' is not just a cliché; it is also a key to victory. Whenever possible, you should scout out the other team and gather whatever intelligence you can find. Your primary goals are to find out the strengths and common strategies of the other team. Based on this information, you can start to form an opinion of the weaknesses of your opponents.

> War is very complicated and confusing. Battle is chaotic. Nevertheless, you must not allow chaos... You must control chaos. This depends upon your planning.
>
> —Sun Tzu, *The Art of War*

Once you have an idea of the other team's strengths and weaknesses, you can design plans that are custom tailored to the game at hand. For example, if you know that the other team has a powerful offense, you may 'overload' your defense when you think that an attack is imminent. The practice of overloading is discussed later in this chapter.

Another topic that is covered later in this chapter is the 'man-to-man' defense. Running that defense is considerably easier if you know the other team. In fact, you could argue that it will only work if you know the other team well enough.

What is the team goal?

The core of your team plan is the overall goal. Just like your individual goals, make your team objectives specific and measurable. 'Get the flag' is an example of a vague goal. It may be measurable but it is so general that it's useless. 'Lockdown the base and then plant the bomb' is a better team goal. However, you could certainly make more specific team goals.

What are the responsibilities of each player?

Each player should understand her responsibilities at all times during the game. This doesn't just mean that she should know her part in the team plan; each player should also understand what to do if the plan goes sour.

The topic of player roles is discussed in detail later in this chapter. A player's role will generally determine her responsibilities.

Have you adapted your plan for the specific game at hand?

Adapting your plan to a team is one important consideration, but it can be just as important to prepare for the game type you are playing. Each game type has its own quirky subtleties that you need to consider. Team strategies for specific game types are covered later in this chapter.

What are your contingency plans?

Planning is an important strength but being inflexible is a painful weakness. Ensure that your team is prepared for the inevitable uncertainty that occurs during a conflict.

Whenever possible, you want to reduce your team's friction and increase the friction for the other team. Even if your plan doesn't work out, you can reduce your own friction by having a well thought out contingency plan.

A team getting ready for the game.

Fighting Positions

One of the most methodical methods for designing contingency plans is to use fighting positions. You should consider investigating fighting positions if you want to orchestrate specific reactions to the ebb and flow of the game.

A fighting position is a location that will provide a player with the best chance to accomplish a task. This may be a position that provides a useful firing line or it could be a concealed location that facilitates an ambush. For example, snipers need a position that gives them a good view of the battlefield, whereas defenders need to cover ingress routes.

It's interesting to note that the Halo 2 artificial intelligence creatures use fighting positions when they are in a battle. This reduces the number of probable locations for the characters in the game and therefore reduces the complexity. In other words, using fighting positions is one of the ways that Bungie increases the performance of Halo 2.

A fighting position doesn't necessarily have to be a camping location; it could be a general area or even a route that favours a player's objective. The *Combat Leader's Field Guide* identifies three types of fighting positions: primary, alternate, and supplemental.

Primary Fighting Position

A primary fighting position is the optimal location for a specific player. Using her primary fighting position, a player is best able to accomplish her task. For example, if a player is defending a bombsite, her fighting position could be a hallway that is likely to be used by the offensive team.

Alternate Fighting Position

An alternate fighting position is a backup location that a player can use to achieve her primary objective. Continuing the example above, an alternate position might be a spot that the player can use if she has to fall back. Her alternate fighting position could be the actual bombsite.

Supplemental Fighting Position

A supplemental fighting position is a location that a player can use to accomplish a goal other than her primary objective. For example, a team defending a flag site might have a plan to play a reverse defense when the game clock reaches twenty seconds. Once the clock ticks down to thirty seconds, players would leave their primary and alternate positions so that they could start fighting from one of their supplemental positions. The reverse defense is discussed in more detail later in this chapter.

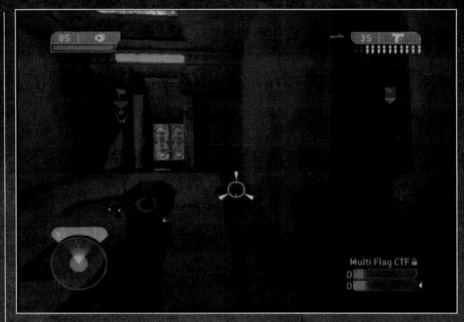

Your primary fighting position must be strong.

An alternate fighting position is a fallback.

A supplementary position helps you achieve a secondary goal.

Two players use mutually supporting positions.

Mutually Supporting Positions

When choosing fighting positions, the optimal strategy is often to establish mutually supporting positions. The idea is simply that two or more players can aid one another by choosing fighting positions that allow them to bring firepower to bear on each other's targets.

These positions often lead to flanking maneuvers or a 'crossfire.' A crossfire is when at least two players are firing ammunition in crossing directions. Whatever is caught in the crossfire is getting at least double the fun.

Crew 116 Advice: Mutually Supporting Positions

Supporting positions are handy for advancing on a less-mobile opponent—for example a sniper, defender, someone who is stuck, or someone who is hiding. One attacker moves up, while the other covers him from a supporting position.

—*char*

You may choose to reject the best possible personal fighting position based on the fact that there is another position that would serve as a better supporting position. Teams will need to weigh the pros and cons when they are deciding whether they can use mutually supporting positions.

Communication

As mentioned earlier in this chapter, one of the most famous causes of battlefield friction is the 'fog of war.' When it comes to Halo 2 matches, your best defense against the fog is to 'talk it up.' Communication is vital to any team game.

The first step to effective team communication is to have a common language for the team. Without common terms for small areas of each map, your team will lack efficient communication. At face value, this may not seem like a big advantage but it is one of the best ways to improve the fluidity of your team. With a common vocabulary, your team will be able to tell one another where things are happening. For example, teams that have been playing Halo 1 a lot will have their own names for most of the rocks on the Halo 1 Blood Gulch level. The figure below demonstrates this point.

In Halo 2, your communication is aided by a few built-in indicators. For example, your Heads up Display (HUD) shows indicators for your teammates. These teammate indicators may decrease the value of team communication, but certainly not completely. When you don't know your teammates, you may have to rely upon feedback such as your teammate indicators.

Some teams choose to ease communication by having one Xbox for the offense and one for the defense. The Crew 116 players even use conference calls so that the offense and defense can talk to one another. While it is true that this could help your team, it may be tough to arrange when playing games over Xbox Live™. However, you may be able to use some sort of voice over IP (VOIP) option. One definite advantage of not relying upon the headsets is that you can talk while you are waiting to spawn. This gives you the chance to immediately update your teammates.

Crew 116 Advice: Team Communication

The point of communication is game knowledge. It's important to know what's happening. Often newbies make the mistake of just chatting or saying random things. That's not helpful to the team.

Information like, "bob's on light ridge", "fred killed me by the port", or "alice is taking a jeep behind our base" is useful information. The goal is to have complete knowledge of where your team is and where the enemy is at all times—to help guide your playing decisions.

Note that this has a solo strategy aspect as well; if you can't keep track of people and pay attention to clues on the map (e.g. rockets are missing), you'll do poorly.

—char

Grassy Knoll
Overshield Cave
Ben's Spot
Death Hill
Dark Ledge
Bread Basket
Cubby Hole
Pistol Cave
Dark Crotch
Powerup
Fragle Rock
Car Point

Fox Spot
Pride Rock
Rockets
Light Crotch

Plateau
Light Ledge
Fuel Rod

Bloodgulch

The Crew 116 vocabulary for the Halo 1 Blood Gulch map.

Attrition Warfare— Or Lack Thereof...

In reality, attrition is a major military consideration. However, in the virtual world of Halo 2, it is not a feasible strategy. Most Halo 2 games allow players to re-spawn infinitely, but this isn't to say that there is no value to a strategy of attrition. Control of a position and possession of weapons and vehicles can be lost when a player is taken out. As you deprive the enemy of their lives, you also deprive them of valuable resources.

For example, if you take out players who have crossed the length of the map, you have taken away the time that it took for them to make the crossing. In addition, you have stolen their weapons and ammunition. A defensive squad can inflict serious damage on an opposing team simply by throwing away their travel time.

If you are playing midfield on a large map—and you have confidence in your team—you may even want to notify your team and let through solitary attackers. By letting the defense handle single attackers, you are spreading out the opposing force. As the players spawn, they may be foolish enough to advance by themselves again. Unless they are smart enough to stop the cycle and attack *en masse*, all they are doing is running down the clock.

The other issue with players spawning over and over is that you will not have much time after defeating players in their own base. Unless you are playing some sort of elimination game, be ready for players to come after revenge.

Weapon Allocation

Weapons may be seemingly abundant in the Halo 2 universe but don't forget that once you have policed a gun, it means that your teammates have to go without that specific weapon for a set period of time. This allocation of weapons can have a huge influence on a game.

Not only should you not hoard weapons but also you should make sure that you leave certain weapons for certain players. You should let team members take the weapons that they use well. For example, the rifles should be reserved for the snipers. In addition, players should do what they can to supply teammates with their allocated weapons and ammunition. If you happen to spawn near a Sniper Rifle, you should consider whether you could take that rifle to your team's snipers.

Little things can also influence the allocation of weapons; for example when you're stuck with a Plasma Grenade you can influence where your weapons land by running in a certain direction.

Don't hoard weapons.

Bodies in the base may mean more players to fight.

Crew 116 Advice: Denying Weapons

When I know that I'm going down, a trick I like to use is to jump off the map to avoid giving my opponent my weapons (e.g. sword or rockets).

—*char*

If you think that you might be temporarily denying the other team's access to a weapon, you might choose to pick it up even if it's just to run it into the shadows. Just bear in mind that you don't want to deliver weapons to the enemy. If you know that you're going to charge into a base, hand off weapons that you won't need. If a team is playing a defense such as zone or choke, you are helping their cause by re-supplying their forces. Zone and choke defenses are discussed later in this chapter.

Playing the Clock

When you're playing defense, diminishing time is your greatest asset. However, when you're on offense, time is an enemy that you can't hold off indefinitely. Watch the game clock so that you don't get surprised when you only have 10 seconds left in the round.

Even if you are not playing a timed game, time is still an invaluable resource to your team. For example, it takes time for players to move to their fighting positions. You are wasting valuable time deploying your forces if your team is constantly getting dropped.

Team Roles

Having roles is part of having an overall team plan. If you're a fan of any team sports, then you know that this is a crucial principle. Without specific objectives, there is far less chance that you will be able to gauge your success with any efficacy. For example, if your role is to defend the flag and the other team scores, then you have failed. At that time, you can ask yourself why you were not able to fulfill your role. Were you outnumbered, outgunned, or outplayed?

In addition, having assigned roles means that you can pay attention to a smaller portion of the battlefield. If chaos erupts far away from your location, you can let the players handling that aspect of the game deal with it.

Crew 116 Advice: Delegation

Delegation is important. We often use a jeep run to try to break a solid lockdown. If the enemy team isn't on the ball, they'll all fall back and try to stop the jeep.

In reality, all it takes is one person normally—but most teams don't realize this and fall back. Ideally, someone says they'll take care of the jeep and everyone else keeps playing their role.

—*char*

When I first played with the members of Crew 116, I had the most trouble during team games. They know their roles inside and out—I didn't have one. I can remember one CTF game where I felt useless; I didn't know where to go or who to engage. This was entirely my fault; in retrospect I should have asked for a specific job to do. It's up to every player to make sure that he has a role and that the rest of the team know what he is going to do.

Crew 116 Advice: Team Roles

On Xbox Live™, I would suggest saying what you're going to do. Telling your teammates lets them know whatever role is covered, and often prompts them to do the same and tell you what they think they're going to do.

Most people are pretty flexible. If something is covered, they can do another job if they know their default choice is taken.

—*char*

General Roles

Assigning a specific role to each player is sometimes not possible. Assigning roles takes time and sometimes you simply don't have the time. For example, the great majority of online team games will use general roles instead of specific roles. When your team is playing general roles, it's still possible for people to assume a specific role, but most of the time you will be playing either 'offense' or 'defense.'

Crew 116 Advice: Xbox Live™ Rounds

Most ranked games have rounds so you'll usually be playing offense or defense. Players will have to be good at both.

That said, you can play 'O' more defensively or 'D' more offensively if you prefer one over the other.

—*char*

Offense

The 'Offense' role is the most common role that players assume. While it is true that the best defense can often be a good offense, make sure that you make this decision consciously. Don't end up with your whole team playing 'O' just because you didn't talk about it.

The players who assume the offensive role should be experts with short-range weapons. The reasons for this are straightforward. First of all, the goal of the offensive player is to get inside the enemy base. Generally speaking, the Halo 2 bases are comprised of small spaces. Therefore, it's often impossible to infiltrate a base using long-range weapons. In addition, if a player defeats an opponent inside the enemy's base, that player will often spawn in close proximity to the attacker.

Crew 116 Advice: Halo 2 Short Range Fights

Halo 2 is more biased towards short range fights than Halo 1. There are fewer ranged weapon spawns, and they do less damage than the Halo 1 pistol.

—*char*

To be effective, players on offense should be well skilled with the short-range DW combos, the Shotgun, and of course, the Plasma Sword. If you're supposed to be playing offense and you find yourself using long-range weapons, you may be playing the 'midfield' role. Keep reading this chapter to find out more about the midfield role.

While it is true that you could be using long-range or mid-range weapons as you approach a target, the offense will generally be forced to fight up close and personal. Work on your short-range skills if you enjoy scoring points.

Players on offense have to get in close.

Defense

I consider myself a defensive specialist; I greatly enjoy shutting down an assault. While it seems that many people get the most pleasure from scoring a flag cap or planting the bomb, I actually enjoy stopping these things from happening. I may not score many points, but I keep the other team from scoring—that's why I play defense. Since few players prefer defense, I generally get to play 'D' whenever I want.

Putting up a strong defense can be as simple as waiting near the objective and fighting in close. This is referred to as 'stay at home D.' This can be a very chaotic role to play, but it can also be great fun. Having players rush in from all sides is messy, but it's also a great way to get in the game. Make sure that you are ready to fight in close if you're going to try this strategy. However, this certainly isn't the only way to stop an attack.

You will be able to see an attack coming if you move outside of the base. This gives you the option of engaging at a distance and warning your team. If you go down far away from your base, you will likely end up spawning in a position to defend the base. This is one of the ways that defense has the advantage.

The astute reader will have noticed that the strategies just described would seemingly favor the defense. If players on the offensive carry only short-range weapons, then they will be vulnerable to the mid-range defensive. This is true; attackers should weigh the risk of being attacked before their objective with the fact that they will eventually have to engage up close. The defense should exploit this dilemma as much as possible.

Midfield

A midfielder must be an expert at prioritizing targets. The reason for this is that the midfielder must support both offensive and defensive maneuvers. Midfielders in a soccer match often have to consider these two conflicting responsibilities. Whether his team is mounting an attack or holding off an assault, the midfielder could be called into action.

If the team is playing without an assigned leader, the midfielder will have to decide when to support the offense and when to support the defense. This decision should be based on the team plan, his own safety, the movements of his opponents, and the information that he gets from his teammates. For example, if the midfielder is taking sniper fire, then he might have to deal with that threat first; however if the other team has the flag, he will have to cover the escape routes.

Based on whom he is supporting, he will usually change his fighting position. However, on a small map, the midfielder may be able to use the same fighting position for both offensive firepower and defensive firepower.

Midfielders are generally expert snipers and strive to play most of the game with a rifle in their hands. At the end of the game, midfielders usually have a high frag count but usually don't score many points. A good midfielder who can score is a valuable find.

Specific Roles

General roles might be enough for strangers on Xbox *Live*™, but they usually aren't the preferred way to plan for a team encounter. When you have the option, your team should use roles that are better targeted to the people and the game that you are playing.

Specific roles become more important as the map gets larger. In a small map, travel times are short so you can more quickly recover from a mistake. When you are on a large map, the time it takes for you to get into position becomes a valuable resource. Specific roles allow you to focus on a specific task and not waste your team's time by running around the map.

The midfield soldier on Zanzibar.

Positional

Players who are assigned positional roles are essentially playing a 'zone defense.' The principle is that some locations on the battlefield are key to the team's plan. The positional player will hold those positions. Locations are significant because of factors such as teleports, powerups, or particular weapons.

A player who is holding an area might be referenced by the name of the area. For example, a player responsible for a teleporter would be called 'the teleporter.' This player essentially guards the teleporter by playing zone defense. Zone defense is covered in more detail later in this chapter.

Weapon

There will be times when a player is given the task of defending a certain weapon or using a certain weapon. This player is often referred to by the name of the weapon. For example, when playing the Rocket Launcher defense, one player will be 'the Rocket Launcher.' The Rocket Launcher defense is discussed later in this chapter. That defense is an example of assigning a weapon to a particular goal and player.

The other type of weapon role is when a player accepts responsibility for guarding a specific weapon. For example, your team might give a particular player the task of removing the threat posed by the enemy with the Rocket Launcher.

That guy is such a camper!

Guarding the Rocket Launcher.

Driver

This role is self-explanatory; the 'driver' is the player who pilots a specific vehicle for a defined purpose. The driver could be skilled with all vehicles, or he may be adept at piloting the ones that happen to be useful on a particular map—or as part of a particular maneuver.

When playing a CTF game, getting the flag carrier into a Warthog can lead to an easy cap. If you are going to try this move, you should make sure that you have a driver who can arrive at the right time and will get the cloth home safely. This means that the driver should have excellent timing and be able to dodge well while in a vehicle.

Another objective that may call for a driver is mounting an assault against a Scorpion tank or Wraith. These vehicles are so powerful that the easiest way to deal with them is usually with another vehicle. Having an expert Banshee pilot can be invaluable when trying to eliminate a tank.

Finding a solid driver is more important than ever now that rockets have vehicle tracking abilities. Whether attacking or defending, a good driver will have to be able to handle rockets homing in on his position.

It is also useful to have a driver with strong jacking skills. It may be necessary for the driver to hijack a ride when called into action.

The driver waiting for the Go/No Go message.

Distraction

Since misdirection is such an effective wartime strategy, players are often asked to take on the role of 'distraction.' The distraction wants every player on the other team to pay attention to him.

The distraction usually wants to make an awful lot of noise and engage as many opponents as possible. To do this, the distraction might drive a tank right up to the enemy base and start pounding away, or he may grab a Sniper Rifle and harass the enemy while he runs around in plain sight. The trouble with being a distraction is that you are inviting firepower to come your way. A good distraction will be able to keep many players busy for an extended period of time. Since the distraction can be more successful if his attackers stay alive, it isn't generally important for him to score many frags.

Some of the best distractions are created by groups of players. The other team believes that they are experiencing a unified maneuver when in reality, they are being kept away from the most dangerous threat.

When faced with favorable terrain, one player might choose to draw fire while his teammates perform a flanking maneuver—this is yet another type of distraction.

When you see a player making a lot of noise and seemingly mounting a suicidal attack, you should ask yourself if he is a distraction.

Just making some noise.

Sneak

The 'sneak' usually doesn't want to make any noise. His goal is to accomplish a task without alerting the other team. A common example of a sneak objective would be to infiltrate the enemy base and grab the flag. However, the sneak might be doing something more subtle such as taking a position so that he can gather reconnaissance. The topic of recon is discussed later in this chapter.

The sneak will often work in coordination with the distraction. The more successful the distraction is, the easier the path for the sneak. For example, the practice of 'spiral misdirection' involves sending a large distraction along one route and a sneak in the opposite direction.

The sneak taking advantage of the distraction.

Leader

There are many quick decisions to be made during the battle. The leader is responsible for making most of these decisions. For example, if your team is preparing for a major offensive, it is up to the leader to give the 'go' signal.

The leader will also assume some other role. Big Team games might seem large but they aren't big enough to have someone sitting on the side lines. The easiest position for the leader to play is midfield, but this isn't a necessity. There will be plenty of decisions made by other players on the team. If the leader is engaged in an attack or defense, some other player will have to step up and make the call.

Examples of decisions that a leader might need to make include the following:

Directing fire: The leader will often take responsibility for the concentration of force on a battlefield. The concept of combined arms is discussed later in this chapter.

Moving forces: A team's ability to maximize firepower is obviously dependant upon the location of players. The leader moves players around the map so that they can participate in offensive and defensive maneuvers.

Changing plans: Not all of your schemes will work out the way that you planned them. When this happens, the leader will issue orders to adjust the changing shape of the battle. In this way, the leader can influence the fluidity of the entire team.

Time to call in some fire.

Time to attack: The greatest organizational challenge in Halo 2 is mounting a team offensive. Not only do you need to position your force, but you also need to ensure that they are properly equipped and that the defense is in a favorable state. The leader should make sure that the players are in position and that they are ready to go.

Calling off an attack: Ironically, some team attacks might be called off because the attacking team's defense has just pulled off a strong victory. For example, let's say that you're playing a Big Team game and getting ready for an offensive. Just before you coordinate your attack, the other team launches a frontal assault with five players. Your defense holds and is able to tag all five attackers. The problem is that these five players spawn close to their base. Instead of facing three defenders, you are now facing eight.

This is an example of a time to call off an attack. The leader should tell his force to hold their posts and wait for the other team to move into a more favorable position.

Lockdown Strategy

During Halo 1 tournaments, 'lockdown' proved to be a dominant strategy. The idea is to control the other team's spawn points such that they aren't able to put up a fight. Before a player is able to move, he is engaged by a better armed opponent. This results in weapon superiority for most fights and a clear disadvantage for the locked down team.

Lockdown is so effective that it can be described as an offensive strategy as well as a defensive strategy. Once a team is locked down, it is much easier to plant a bomb or steal a flag. However, it is also impossible for a team to wage an offense if they are fully locked down.

When your team is locked down, it can be incredibly frustrating. Sometimes you will barely take a step before getting shot and other times you will spawn with a grenade landing at your feet. Locked down players will often use a quick melee to move their head just as they spawn. This may be enough to dodge a sniper bullet, but it's a momentary respite from a painful situation.

Keep in mind that teams will often forego their main objective until they are able to accomplish the lockdown. For example, during a King of the Hill (KotH) game, the Crew 116 team was able to rack up over four minutes in a five-minute game. The other team would hide and not engage, and generally play strangely. They were trying to gain control of the Human Pistol. The strategy worked; they eventually outfitted their whole team with pistols. Despite dying a lot, the other team managed to get lockdown. They eventually dethroned Crew 116 from the hill. After that, they controlled the pistol spawn and the hill. Despite a four-minute lead, Crew 116 lost the game.

If you feel that lockdown strategies are unethical, refer to Chapter 10, Essential Halo 2 Etiquette. Remember that a winning team will use any technique allowed in the current game.

Team Offense

Many game types simply cannot be won without waging effective offensive operations. While your team might be able to win a Team Slayer game by using an effective defensive stance, your team will certainly not be able to win a CTF game by hanging back the whole game.

Even in a game with strangers, you will want to try to coordinate your offensive strikes. The fact is that defense is easier to arrange without preparation. Defenders can check the important access routes to see if someone on their team is covering the vulnerability. If a defender finds an entry that is unguarded, then it's safe to say that defending that access point is going to be a good fighting position for that defender.

In contrast, the offense must at least coordinate when their team will attack. Sometimes just getting the entire assault team ready to attack can be a challenge. If you don't know your teammates, use the team channel to organize your offense.

Frontal Assault

The frontal assault is the most basic offense. Simply gather the largest possible offensive force and rush the objective together. These attacks are not exactly the pinnacle of strategy but that does not mean that you should never use them.

If you believe that you have an advantage, then a frontal assault can be quick and effective. In short timed games a frontal assault is often used as part of a larger plan. For example, you might rush the other team's base knowing that a sneak is going to be bringing the bomb. Just remember that even a frontal assault should be coordinated. If you are going to try to use brute force, then you want the greatest force possible behind your maneuver.

By launching a full offensive you can weaken the other team just enough to give your other plans a chance to succeed. Of course, frontal assaults are also used in desperation when time is running down. Try to avoid getting your team into that precarious situation.

To facilitate a large assault, you will want to organize your forces at a designated staging area. The staging area allows your entire team to start an assault at the same time. Generally, you will want to meet at a secure location near the target. However, if you are using vehicles, you could be further away.

Go, go, go!

Crew 116 Advice: Frontal Assault

Timing is the key to a successful attack. The easiest way to manage your timing is to use a safe staging area that is near the target.

—DJ 116

Overload

Athletes who play team sports know all about overload strategies. The idea is simple; shift your attack so that you outnumber the enemy. Regardless of how many defenders are guarding, the attacking team can mount an overloaded attack if they have at least one more player than the defense.

Generally, the defensive side will choose fighting positions that give them views of all the possible attack routes. The offense can exploit this fact by combining their arms and targeting one or two ingress paths. The concept of 'combined arms' is discussed later in this chapter.

For example, let's say that you are playing a Small Team assault game on the Ivory Tower level. Your team spawns at the elevator and you need to plant the bomb near the courtyard. At first, you send two two-person fire teams in opposite directions. Squad A is carrying the bomb and Squad B is going to overload the defense. Squad B is given a slight lead so that they are the first group to encounter the defense.

In our scenario the defense has been deployed in the most common formation—they are camping the bombsite. They have two players on each side of the bomb, one above on the wooden level and one on ground level.

Offensive Squad B comes out of the basement and causes a distraction on their side of the map. This could be as simple as firing at the enemy or chucking a grenade. The defense may decide to shift their forces to deal with the immediate threat; if they do so the offense has an easier time with their overload move.

Let's say that the defense shifts one player over to the distraction. They are now engaging two attackers with three defenders—they are trying a defensive overload. This is the tricky part for the offense. Squad B needs to keep the defense contained and break across the courtyard to join Squad A. Simultaneously, Squad A comes around the corner and the attackers now have four players against one. The bomb should have a decent approach to the bombsite.

Of course, all of this happens in a matter of seconds. If the offense didn't move quickly enough, they would simply get entangled with the defenders and not have a chance to make a move.

Crew 116 Advice: Why Overload Can Work

Almost no one changes their mind after they have engaged. For example, once a defender goes to the other side of the map, there's little chance he's coming back before his opponents are eliminated. Human psychology I suppose—but it's why the distraction technique is so powerful.

People seem to give in to their bloodlust. Merely saying, "Hi, I'm over here" is often enough to pull the entire team in that direction.

—char

I'm guessing that the question on your mind is 'why doesn't the 'D' just shift with the attackers?' This is where the chaos of the situation aids the attacking team. The defense should shift position, but by that time the offense already has accomplished their goal. Even if one of the attackers is fragged from behind, the offense will still overload the defense. Either the bomb is planted or it's right near the site.

Performing the overload maneuver on Ivory Tower.

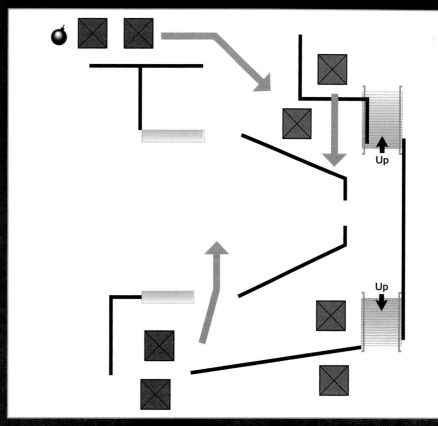

Before the overload maneuver.

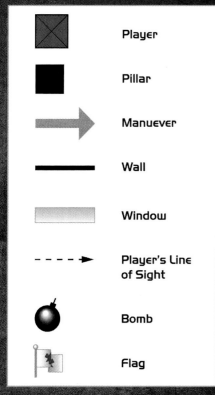

	Player
	Pillar
	Manuever
	Wall
	Window
	Player's Line of Sight
	Bomb
	Flag

Maneuvers legend.

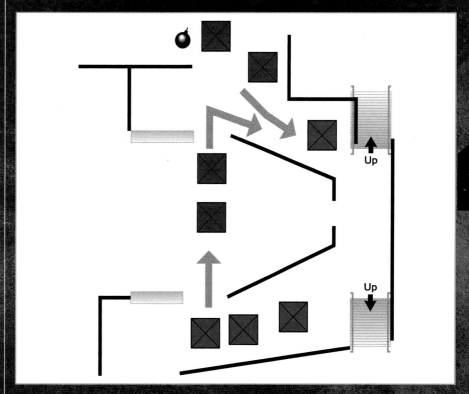

An offensive overload maneuver.

Pressing the Rocket Launcher

There are numerous defensive strategies that rely upon a linchpin element—for example, the Rocket Launcher defense which is discussed later in this chapter. When a team is using a weapon or a location to their advantage, an obvious counter to their plan is to 'press' that element.

In the case of the Rocket Launcher defense, the attacking team throws people at the problem until it is neutralized. Either the offensive team will take out the threat or they will exhaust his ammunition. Either way, the defensive team will have to change their strategy. By pressing the player with the launcher, the offense is using yet another type of overload strategy.

This strategy assumes that the offense has time to mount at least two attacks and that they can prevent the other team from getting more rockets. However, on the Ivory Tower level, this isn't difficult to do.

Not much ammo left.

Vehicle Attacks

Many team games include vehicles. Although they are often used to fight back attackers or lock down a base, they can also be used for specific strategic strikes.

The best example of this has to be using a Warthog to drive home a captured flag. Once you have a flag carrier in a moving jeep, it is extremely difficult for the defense to stop you. Unless they happen to be using a reverse defense, they will probably not be able to save the cap. The reverse defense is discussed later in this chapter.

Knowing that vehicles can be so important, make sure that your team has a plan for their use and deployment.

When first playing Zanzibar, I found that most attackers jumped into the vehicles right away and staged a rolling frontal assault. It didn't take very long before the defense used the Rocket Launcher to halt this offensive tactic. Again, the other team reacted and the offense stopped using vehicles in their first attack. It was then that an interesting thing happened; the defense generally adopted the Rocket Launcher defense inside the Zanzibar base. Logically, the offensive side should have adapted and kept the defense honest by reinstating vehicle attacks. Without the threat of a locked-on rocket, they could bring a Puma right up to the Zanzibar base. Strangely, this didn't happen. Players became so frightened of the Rocket Launcher that they didn't get back in the saddle.

Use your vehicles.

Air Support

When you find that you're playing in a game with Banshees, you should consider whether air support could affect your strategy. There are clearly two situations that you must consider. The first is whether using air support could help your team. There will be cases where it isn't necessary. Secondly, you must ask yourself whether air support could put a halt to your plans. In other words, if the enemy uses a Banshee, will they have an easier time shutting you down?

If you feel that Banshees will play a role in the game, you should police them prior to launching any major maneuvers. If you are going to use a Banshee, keep it out of harm's way until you are ready to go. If you don't want the other team to have one, then send out a search and destroy team with the Rocket Launcher. You may want to plan to launch your attack as soon as the Banshee is blown out of the sky.

Using Overtime

Keep in mind that many team games have an overtime feature. For example, if you are playing CTF, the game will not end if the offense has a player close enough to the flag. Merely touching the flag will reset the game time to five seconds. When you are playing offense, overtime is your friend.

Rather than rush a flag at the end of the game, spread out your players so that there is constantly someone getting near the flag. You can extend a round for a considerable time using this strategy.

Support your infantry.

The offense gets the glory...

Team Defense

The tough part of defense is maintaining the initiative. Generally, you're reacting to attackers, but don't think that this means that you should simply accept what they throw at you. Defenders should be constantly searching for ways to blast holes through the offensive strategy.

On small maps, defenders have little time to react and shift their firepower. However, these types of situations tend to illicit complacency in the offensive side. They figure that it's a twitch map so they will just use frontal attacks until they attain lockdown. If you are playing 'D' you can exploit this attitude.

For example, on the lockout level, players assume that they will find defenders camping out on the flag spot. Instead of doing so, immediately stage an aggressive counterattack and then play a reverse defense. Reverse defense is discussed later in this section.

...but defense wins the game.

Defensive Action

The *Combat Leader's Field Guide* outlines the following actions as the fundamentals of mounting a defense:

1. **Prepare for combat.**
2. **Move to defensive positions.**
3. **Establish defensive positions.**
4. **Locate the enemy and take action on enemy contact.**
5. **Fight the defense.**
6. **Reorganize.**

The defense may decide to adjust after a successful battle.

This may seem like a facile list but it is valuable to stress the importance of reorganization. Just because your first defensive stand was successful, it doesn't mean that your second one will be as effective.

In addition, you can use reorganization to fool the offense into focusing their effort on the wrong sector of the map. If you shift your defense mid-game, you may find that you surprise the offense. 'Focus of effort' is discussed later in this chapter.

Rocket Launcher Defense

An effective defensive strategy is to let your opponents get near their objective (e.g. flag or bombsite) and then smack them with a rocket. In quick matches, this can be especially effective because the lack of abundant rocket ammo will not be such an issue. If you are able to stop a single full attack, then this strategy has paid off.

This strategy was very popular on Zanzibar. Rather than use the Rocket Launcher to counter vehicle attacks, the defensive team would keep the launcher in the base and destroy players as they tried for the flag.

As mentioned above, the offensive side rarely adjusted to this strategy. Whereas the offense was usually apprehensive about using vehicles, the rocket defense allowed the attacking team to drive right up to the base. The best counter for this defense would be to press the Rocket Launcher until he is out of the picture or runs out of ammo. Once the Rocket Launcher is gone, the attackers can grab the flag and hop into a hog waiting just outside the base.

It just doesn't seem fair.

Reverse Defense

This idea may seem backwards, but that's the point. Instead of defending the beginning of the enemy's objective, your team catches the enemy off guard by defending the end of the objective.

Most CTF games have a clear beginning goal and end goal. The attacking team must first get the flag and then they must transport it back to their base for the cap. A team playing a reverse defense would abandon the flag and slip through the enemy's lines. Once the other team

tried to return with the flag, the defensive side would have assumed fighting positions in their opponent's base.

The reverse defense can be particularly effective on a map such as Zanzibar where the beach flag spot can be defended with Ghosts. If this strategy is successful, it's easy for the defense to then switch to a lockdown strategy.

Remember that strategies should be combined when possible. For example, you may want to have a portion of your force play the Rocket Launcher defense and the rest assume a reverse defense.

A reverse defense setup.

Full Court Press

This is a full counterattack strategy. The plan is to get to the other team's base and take them out before they have a chance to arm themselves. Once you have run the full court press, you may decide to use a reverse defense or go for lockdown.

The key to this strategy is that the offense will usually take for granted that they can move to certain locations without engaging any defenders. Using this strategy, you surprise the enemy and aim to eliminate them before they are ready to mount an attack.

Man-to-Man

I have to admit that I haven't heard of anyone running this defense in a Halo 2 game. However, I will include it because it contrasts nicely with the next topic—zone defense.

Man 'D' is when you assign certain defenders to specific attackers; it's a common basketball strategy. Your goal is to match up players in a way that you believe will give you a big advantage. For example, if you know that the other team has one elite player, you will probably want your best player to cover him. However, if you believe that you can use a

defensive specialist against their top player, this may free up your star player to move against a lesser player. This results in mismatch and is your ticket to victory.

This type of strategy would be tough to use on a small map. In addition, there are certain game types that favor man defense. For example, territory games are an excellent candidate for this defense. If you can deploy your mid-level players so that they occupy the stars of the other team, then you are giving your best players a chance to shine.

Using stolen Zanzibar vehicles for a full court press.

Crew 116 Advice: Man-to-Man Defense

One of the few times man-to-man works well is when two groups collide. For example, I'm playing on the same team as Bob and we run into two enemies. If we quickly decide to play 'man', Bob can quickly eliminate their lesser player while I keep their better player occupied—then it's a two-on-one with their remaining man.

—char

Zone

Zone is the complete opposite of man-to-man defense. Instead of assigning defenders to specific players, you assign defenders to sectors of the map. Positional roles are an example of running zone defense.

The advantages of zone defense include the fact that your team doesn't need to know where the attackers are located. It simply doesn't matter—your players just go out to their fighting positions and hold a location. Once the attackers have engaged, effective team communication should allow your whole team to know where most of the attackers are located.

Holding a zone may not be easy; you may find that some players end up running out of ammunition. If you are running this defense, you need to pay attention to weapon allocation. Hopefully, your team will start off well-equipped and the enemy will deliver supplies.

An obvious counter to zone defense is an overload attack. Having a number of players run in a 'wolf pack' through the zones can mean that the offense constantly outnumbers the defenders.

Choke Point

Guarding choke points is a specific type of zone defense. Instead of guarding a patch of ground, you are covering an entrance, hallway, or tunnel—any space that is tight and will be used by invaders.

This defense facilitates successful ambushes. Just make sure that you know if the other team is using a different route.

Guarding a choke point.

Reverse Slope Defense

This classic military defense works on the principle that soldiers expect hilltops to be the fighting ground. Since playing the high ground is an advantage, a fixed defensive location is usually at the top of a hill. However, the reverse slope defense is designed to ambush people as they move over the crest of a hill that they believe is not defended. It's an effective surprise attack.

Waiting for opponents to come over the crest of a hill.

One aspect of this particular surprise is that the enemy cannot see where you have placed your forces. You could have a single sniper or a Scorpion waiting.

The Crew 116 version of this defense is to have a distraction pull people in by sticking her head over the hill. Once she has attracted a victim, a sniper is there to take him out. Some people call this move a 'bait and switch ambush.'

A bait and switch ambush.

More Military Strategy for Halo 2

Bonnini's paradox states that as a simulation approaches reality, the complexity of the model decreases the value of the simulation. However, this principle obviously doesn't apply to the enjoyment of video games. Since Bungie has done such an amazing job on the Halo 2 engine, you can apply real-world military strategy to the Halo 2 universe.

If you do not believe that real world strategies can work in a video game, then ask yourself why the United States military has spent millions of dollars on video games. The video game 'America's Army' was funded by the United States military. The military is willing to spend the money because they have established that soldiers benefit from practicing their techniques in the virtual world. You can benefit from the reciprocal—learn from soldiers and apply their strategies to Halo 2.

Pincer Attack

The pincer attack is a classic flanking maneuver. Rather than one force flanking the enemy, two forces flank from different directions. This maneuver can be devastating because the target will often be completely exposed on one side.

Performing this maneuver is fairly simple; all you need is a nimble two-player fire team. The pair either sets up an ambush or moves to engage an enemy from two different attack angles.

The diagram in the upper right of this page shows a pincer attack. The victim of the attack may be able to take partial cover but the multi-directional attack leaves him vulnerable from at least one side.

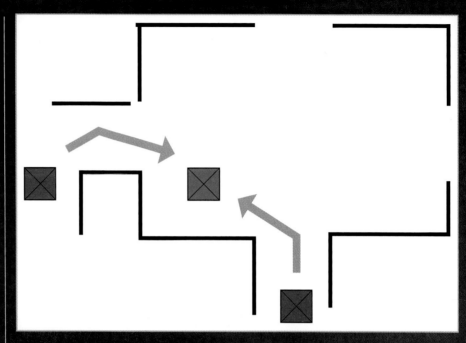

A pincer attack.

Executing the same pincer maneuver.

Enveloping Maneuver

Enveloping is the most lethal form of flanking maneuver. The goal of this attack is to surround the enemy and engage simultaneously from multiple firing positions. The enemy has little chance of escape or survival.

The diagram in the lower right of this page demonstrates an enveloping attack.

Executing the enveloping maneuver.

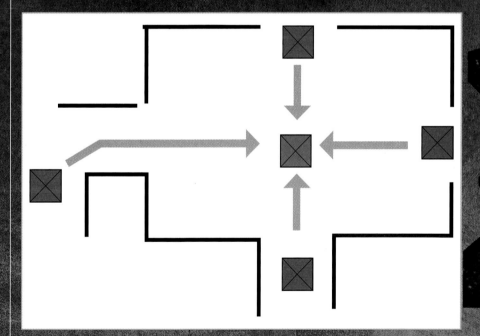

An enveloping maneuver.

Shaping the Battle

One way to control the battlefield is to exploit interior and exterior lines. An interior line is the boundary of your secure territory; an exterior line marks the enemy's territory. As forces move around the map, these lines shift. *Warfighting* refers to this struggle as 'shaping the battle.'

Using lines of attack, you can methodically move your team across a map. If you are aiming for a lockdown, then this is a great way to deploy your forces. Remember that a longer line is a weaker line. When your team is in motion, you may have to shift players across your line so that they can support other players who have engaged the enemy.

This diagram shows interior and exterior lines on the Zanzibar map.

Here is a screenshot of the same interior and exterior lines.

Interior and exterior lines in Halo 2.

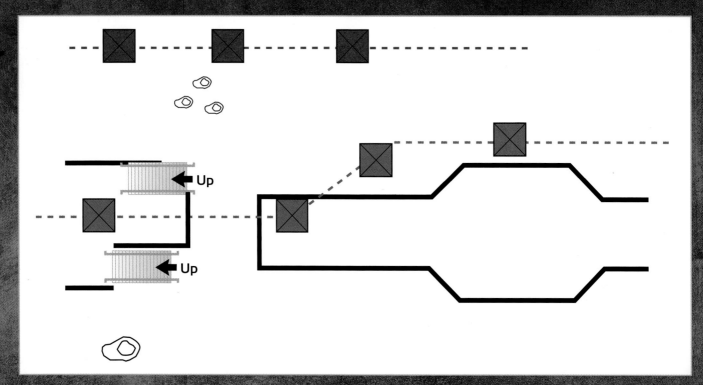

A diagram of interior and exterior lines.

Battle of the Bulge

If you can predict or quickly recognize the fighting lines, then you can perform maneuvers that will break the enemy lines. A successful break in a line forms the shape of a 'bulge.' If you are on offense, a bulge is an opportunity to flank your enemy. You can do this by having the players in the bulge double back to one side. This will trap a portion of the exterior line in an enveloping maneuver. If your line is broken by a bulge, then you must retreat or counterattack.

This figure shows a bulge in fighting lines.

If a single player is able to break through your line, you might want to run an enveloping maneuver to stop the threat. However, if the attacking team is organized, the breaking player will have proper firepower support.

The same 'bulge' in the interior line.

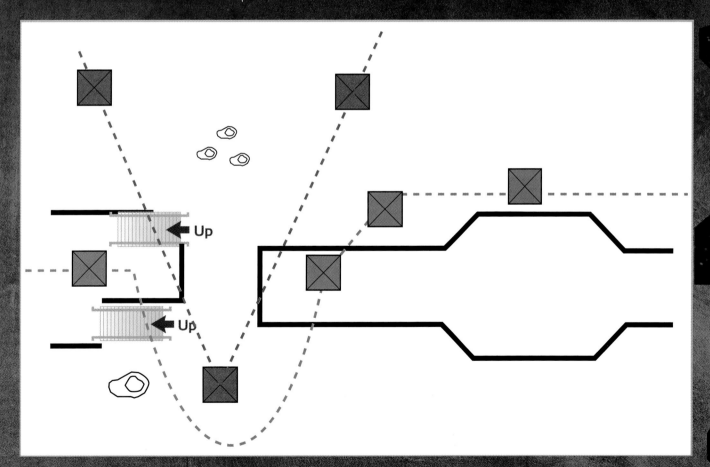

A diagram of a 'bulge' in the interior line.

Focus of Effort

Focus is all about attention. In terms of warfare, the 'focus of effort' is maintained when players are paying attention to the most important objective at each moment. It isn't sufficient to understand the ultimate goal of the game. As was already noted, 'winning the game' is not a specific enough goal. Through excellent planning and effective communication, you should keep your focus of effort on the immediate objective. If you are using fighting lines, a bulge should grab your attention.

Combined Arms

When you carefully allocate your resources on a map, it is known as 'economy of force.' The primary goal of economy of force is to focus your strength on the activities that require the most firepower. When your team is launching a campaign, make sure that you are combining your arms in the right way. For example, are you using mutually supporting fighting positions?

When it comes to vehicle warfare, combining your arms is essential to success. Since there are so few vehicles, you need to be especially careful with their deployment.

Use the big guns where you need them the most.

Ambush

The ambush is the most famous military surprise attack. Whether you are playing offense or defense you should consider whether an ambush is right for your game plan. Of course, small ambushes are the bread and butter of any good Halo 2 player. For example, when a strong player comes across a battle, he will often wait for the two combatants to weaken each other and then run in for the double kill.

Many fighting positions are chosen because they will be good spots to launch an ambush. One thing to remember about Halo 2 ambushes is that they could come from any direction. A Banshee could swoop down from above, a player could use an air vent, or someone could drop in at the most unexpected time. When you learn the Halo 2 maps, you should also learn the best ambush locations.

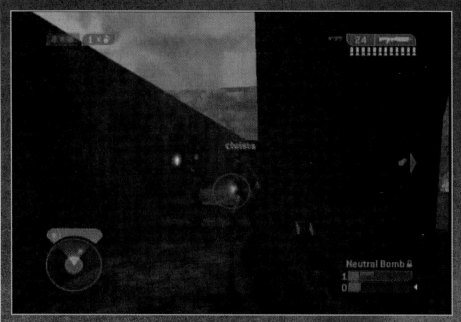

Just a little closer.

Reconnaissance

In the Halo 2 arsenal, one of the underrated weapons is reconnaissance. If your team wants to do everything possible to ensure success, then you should consider whether a recon patrol could be useful.

Some strategies can benefit a great deal from reconnaissance. For example, flanking maneuvers require that you know exactly where the enemy is located. Decide whether you could use some intelligence when you plan a maneuver. If the situation is right, you may want to send in a sneak to get the lay of the land.

> **Look, instead of just running straight into enemy gunfire like we usually do, why don't we try some reconnaissance?**
> **—Griff from Red vs. Blue** (http://www.redvsblue.com)

A solitary recon maneuver.

A recon soldier supporting his team.

Sample Team Game Type Strategies

Team Slayer Strategy

Just like single player FFA, Team Slayer is a race to get a certain number of frags. The first team to get to the goal wins.

In a Team Slayer game, a 16-player game with two teams can be thought of as a two person FFA game. Each time you get killed, it's like everyone on the other team just got a point. For this reason, you should not be as aggressive during Team Slayer matches. Having a brick on your team can be a real boost to the other team's score.

Team Slayer is a conflict between chaos and teamwork.

Wolf Packs

When a team travels together, this is referred to as a 'wolf pack.' This can be an effective Team Slayer or Territory strategy. When the wolf pack runs into single players, the solo fighters don't have a chance. However, there are issues with this practice. Bunching together makes it easier for the opposing team to get a multiple kill or perform a flanking maneuver on the whole team.

In addition, if your opponents have rockets, it becomes important to space your team wisely. If you are in a wolf pack, stay close but not too close.

I didn't score that many killtaculars but I remember one in particular that was especially rewarding. I was playing a one-flag CTF game on the Lockout map. The other team had managed to get the flag all the way down from the tower and into the room with the lift. However, they

Crew 116 Advice: Team Slayer Strategy

Map dominance is critical. Get position, get weapons, and get control. If you're behind in kills, play smart and avoid fights until you're rearmed and in a good position. This is one of the games that's worth practicing so you understand when to run and when to fight.

—char

Team Slayer is all about controlling the resources. Your team needs to be capable of protecting and/or obtaining any item that could change the tide of the match. Typically, the crucial items are: powerups, Rocket Launcher, Sniper Rifle. Some maps and game types feature reduced weapon sets, or are designed to make normally commonplace equipment hard to obtain. For example, in Halo 1, if there was only one player with a Human Pistol, that player could be very powerful.

—Striker

Find an area that's defensible and get long range weapons. Then pick the enemy off as they try (or don't try) to come at you.

—tantrum

Always be within eyesight of teammates but not right next to each other. Close means that you can help each other; too close means that you could all be taken out with a single rocket. Secure high ground and ranged weapons at all costs.

—DJ 116

Most people seem to think that running in packs is the best strategy; I tend to disagree. I think two people coming from different directions works much better. When you travel in groups, that just means my grenades do more damage. I like to be a distraction as my teammate comes from behind and lays everybody to waste.

—MrJukes

made the mistake of traveling too close together. Even though it was four against one, I was able to mow down the other team with ease.

The reason for this was certainly not my fighting skills; it was the fact that all four of my enemies were running in file up the ramp to the lower flag spot. I simply fought them in order and if they tried to combine their arms, all they did was hit each other in the back. They had brought down

each other's shields and I was able to cut through for the killtacular. If any one of those players had hung back just a little bit, he would have easily been able to take me down and grab the flag. After the battle, the time expired before they could score the cap.

A Small Team wolf pack.

CTF Strategy—Capture the Flag

Halo 2 contains more asymmetric maps than Halo 1 and online Halo 2 CTF is usually played in rounds. When you play asymmetric maps it is more common to either be playing offense or defense. For these reasons, Halo 2 concentrates on one flag CTF, whereas Halo 1 focused on two flag CTF. Most of the strategies described here are relevant to one flag CTF.

One thing to remember is that you have the option to drop the flag forward to run faster. However, when you do this, there is an announcement and a visual indicator where it lands. The trick is that if the other team already knows where the flag is, you may as well drop and run. If you do decide to use this tactic, remember that the flag has some weird physics associated with it. It may end up moving in a way that you didn't expect.

Supporting the flag carrier on Ivory Tower.

Defending a flag spot.

Crew 116 Advice: General CTF

Throwing jeeps at the enemy is something I think is very valuable. On offense, you pull them into their base and leave transport at their base. On defense, you pull them away from your base.

—tantrum

Crew 116 Advice: CTF Offense

The most effective strategy is to control the spawn points. In other words, to get 'lockdown.' Most Capture the Flag games have 'bases' and the players spawn near these bases. Some people might have an issue with spawn camping, but it really is the most effective way to get control of a base (and deliver the bomb or grab the flag). Other techniques involve distraction. Make a big ruckus on one side of the map, draw the defenders toward that side, and then send someone in from the other side. This works particularly well for assault games.

—char

Use "the backdoor attack". Immediately grab the flag and run it along a roundabout route such that it is out of the way, and out of sight from the enemies. As they concentrate on running their own flag, sneak the flag into the lightly guarded base. The best Halo 1 example of this was on Battle Creek when playing as Blue. You can take the flag out the side exit from the basement, and up the ladder to the sniper perch. From there you can jump to the rocket ledge, and then a perfect jump will land you on top of the Red base. You can then easily score from the hole in the top of the base by dropping down and crouching on the platform above the flag spot. This same route works if you are attacking the Red base—in that case, crouching picks up the flag. You then need to jump out the side window of the Red base and head for the teleporter in the back.

—Striker

Sometimes all you have to do is lockdown ranged weapons and then push your entire team at the flag.

—DJ 116

Pound, pound, pound! Carry the flag back to your spawn ten feet at a time. Even if you just pick up the flag to prevent it from resetting you have done a good job. For games with touch return on, it's generally a good idea to either use vehicles or to travel in a group. Also, it's fairly easy for a good defense to pick you off if you stream into the base one at a time. A well-coordinated attack from multiple directions is always the best strategy.

—MrJukes

Crew 116 Advice: CTF Defense

Don't let them anywhere near your base. Obviously, combining these strategies for offense and defense implies there's a big battle for the midfield; it's the staging ground for pushing up to either team's base. Good sniping is critical in most team games. Prioritizing threats is imperative for the sniper, and he should focus on helping support the offensive or defensive push—not randomly shoot at people who happen to be in their reticle.

—char

Defenders have to ensure that while they are locking down the base, no straggling enemies have slipped past them. A lone enemy at your base can wait and kill the flag carrier as he tries to score, or make a quick attempt at the unguarded flag.

—Striker

Split up to get ranged weapons and take out any player that pushes too close. Kill players with ranged weapons before worrying about getting the flag back. Defending a CTF game should always involve someone sticking near the flag. Try to get rockets or shotguns to roam near the flag. Have the rest of the team set up a small perimeter—they need to be close enough to fall back if one side of the defense fails.

—DJ 116

Cover all the choke points. Every map has choke points. These are places the enemy must travel through in order to reach your base. Control those points and you will win. If everybody just sits back in the base and waits for the enemy to grab the flag, they will just pound the flag home. You have to kill them before they can even get close to the base.

—MrJukes

Assault Strategy

Assault is a popular team game. The goal is to transport a bomb to the other team's base and arm it. For many people, it is a perfect mix of the strategy of CTF and the chaos of Slayer. When playing assault, you must remember a few crucial points:

Planting the bomb isn't the ultimate goal.

Planting the bomb is not enough to win the game. However, many players will move as if it's the only consideration. Remember that you're playing as part of a team, so make sure that the bombsite is defensible when you plant the bomb.

Even if the defense outnumbers the invaders, a bomb can be defended with some well-timed grenade throws and sniper rounds.

The bomb will eventually return if dropped.

Just like the flag, the bomb will usually return after a specified period of time. Remember that it may be worth a life to just pick up the bomb and drop it.

An exploding bomb.

Crew 116 Advice: Assault Strategy

Assault is one of the games where being sneaky can pay off. In CTF, you need to get the flag (big announcement to everyone) and get out. That's certainly harder than just running the bomb into the base. A good jeep run can deliver the bomb quickly and provide 1-2 more players to support the push in the base. The lone man running in the bomb can also work.

Feints work well. Try attacking in strength from one direction and sneak the bomb in from the other. Sometimes an early rush in a jeep can also be effective (for example, on the Waterworks map). Pile in and blitz to the other side of the map—while the opponents are getting weapons and messing around in the base. At times, you can score a quick cap. It works well on noobs, but sometimes surprises even experienced players.

—char

Camping in the base can be useful. For example, on Zanzibar it's the only way to win. The most effective offensive assault strategy I've seen is misdirection—send the bomb and an escort one way, and many noise makers the other way. It's hard not to fall for that.

—tantrum

Leave the bomb at your base until your team can open up an alley for attack. Do not approach the base with the bomb until your teammates give the go-ahead.

In assault games, the timer does not run down to 0 if the bomb is held. Use this "overtime" to your advantage. If you are short on time, have a player hold the bomb while the rest of the team clears the way to the opponent's base.

Of course, communication is crucial. Defending an assault game is all about finding the bomb. Coordination is key. On defense, set up a wide perimeter and spread out as far as you can while still keeping line of site (so nobody can sneak through). Once you have a visual on the bomb, the entire team can collapse on it. Once you own the bomb, send a player or two to attack the bomb spawn location since you know that's where it will go next.

—DJ 116

Once the bomb is planted, carpet bomb the area until it detonates. Having a sniper pick off people trying to diffuse never hurts either. On defense, track down the bomb and take it out before it gets close to the plant site. Once the bomb is down, don't let them pick it up again. Don't be afraid to camp the bomb—it's your objective. Also be mindful of that little bomb reset timer.

—MrJukes

King of the Hill

The goal of KotH games is to accumulate a specified amount of time on the 'hill'. The hill is clearly visible to everyone via a navigation marker and a glowing crown- shaped effect on your screen.

When playing hill games, it's important to have people protecting the routes to the hill. Mounting a choke defense will prevent the other team from getting close enough to challenge the King.

You only need one player on the hill.

Territories

This game is similar to territories in Myth®. There are a number of 'territories' on the map and you get time for controlling them. Controlling a territory means your flag is there. Contested territories yield no time. It takes a few seconds of standing in the territory to plant your flag, and a few seconds to take away an enemy flag. Time accrues for every territory you own. For example, if you hold two territories then you will be gaining twice the time.

In territory games, either take a strong defensible position with the majority of the flags or overwhelm one and then move to the next. Hopefully the other team will be playing catch-up the whole game.

SPARTANs guarding their territory.

Crew 116 Advice: Territories

There are two main strategies in this game. The first is to have one person solely control a territory. This only works if you have a really strong player and he can find a defensible territory. The counter to this strategy is to envelop the defender.

The second strategy is to occupy a territory *en masse*. Get everyone together and roll around the map taking enemy territories. If your opponents are disorganized, they'll keep losing territories. If you take them faster than the other teams can take them back, then you will do well. The counter to this method is to split up and take undefended territories.

—*char*

Additional Reading

If you are interested in reading more about the philosophy and strategy of warfare, I recommend that you take a look at these books. Of course, these books were written for non-virtual combat so a lot of the information is inapplicable.

Combat Leader's Field Guide
by MSG Brett A. Stoneberger, Stackpole Books
ISBN 0-8117-2729-7

This is the most technical of the three books recommended. It includes specific maneuvers with detailed diagrams.

The Art of War
by Sun Tzu

This is one of the most famous books about military strategy. Written roughly 2,400 years ago, it continues to be a popular strategy book for warfare and business. There are various editions of this book, but I recommend the following:

The Art of War, Plus The Ancient Chinese Revealed
Gary Gagliardi
ISBN 1929194196

Warfighting, The U.S. Marine Corps Book of Strategy
The United States Marine Corps
ISBN 0-385-47834-8

This book focuses on the philosophy of warfare.

Chapter 8: Multiplayer Maps

> "Next is the terrain.
>
> It can be distant or near.
>
> It can be difficult or easy.
>
> It can be open or narrow.
>
> It also determines your life or death."
>
> —Sun Tzu, *The Art of War*

As you have learned throughout this guide, weapon superiority determines the outcome of many fights. If for no other reason than to arm yourself, you should make yourself familiar with the multiplayer maps. Some maps are a rush for weapons. If you know the precise location of every weapon on the map, you will know where to run as soon as you spawn.

There are other reasons to familiarize yourself with the terrain. You also want to know the location of things such as the powerups, teleporters, useful jumps, and obviously the bases.

Furthermore, players who know the lay of the land will be best prepared to create their own tactics and strategies for each map.

Practice Tip:

If you're serious about learning a map, try running around it backwards. This will pay huge dividends when you're able to defend your backside as you retreat.

Ascension

Size: Small

Ideal Number of Players: 2–8

Vehicles Supported: Banshee

Targeted Game Types: 1-on-1, Juggernaut, Oddball, Slayer

Territories: Command Center, Dish, Landing Pad, Leap of Faith, Sniper Roost

Features: Small area with a single Banshee.

Default Weapons:

Magnum Pistol

Shotgun

Battle Rifle

Sniper Rifle

Rocket Launcher

Fragmentation Grenades

Plasma Pistol

Needler

Plasma Grenades

Details: This level looks like a floating rock with an unfinished building on top. Of course, it's actually part of the Forerunner machinery for the Halo systems.

The level is relatively small but whoever gets the lone Banshee will have plenty of space.

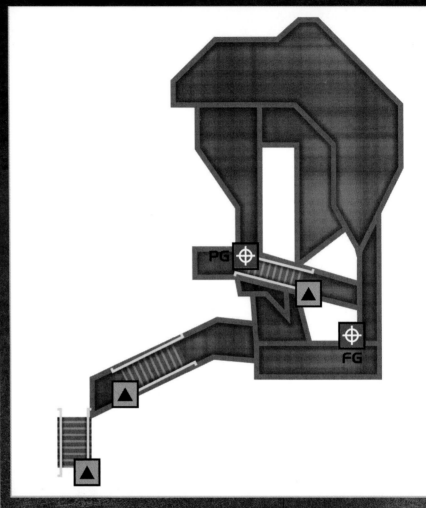

Ascension upper level.

LEGEND

⬍		Elevator	⊕		Weapons
✳		Exploding Container		MP	Magnum Pistol
				SU	Sub Machine Gun
⬏ ⬐		Flag		SH	Shotgun
)))		Lift		BA	Battle Rifle
				SR	Sniper Rifle
⚙		Mechanism		RL	Rocket Launcher
⚡		Powerup		FG	Fragmentation Grenades
▲		Ramp		PP	Plasma Pistol
				PR	Plasma Rifle
⊟		Teleporter		PS	Plasma Sword
				NE	Needler
⊤		Turret		CC	Covenant Carbine
				BR	Beam Rifle
◉		Vehicles		BS	Brute Shot
				PG	Plasma Grenades

Multiplayer maps legend.

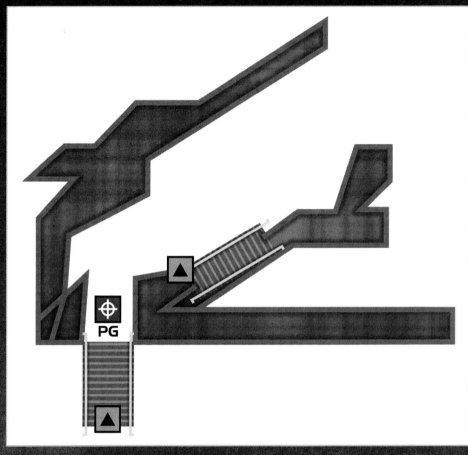

Ascension Low Tower Side View

Crew 116 Advice: Ascension

I can't believe they left the Banshee on this map for FFA. Since it's fairly open, ranged weapons are great on this map. There are a couple of trick jumps I've found so far—I'm sure there are more. It's a small map that will be fun for 1v1 (without the Banshee of course).

—char

I think that aside from the Banshee/rocket combo, this is largely a sniper map. There's one rifle for each tower, and a good sniper with radar on can do a lot of damage. I would choose that (sniper plus shotgun to gank those that come over to kill me) over the battle rifle. Also interesting to note that it's pretty easy to throw nades up into the sniper tower.

—tantrum

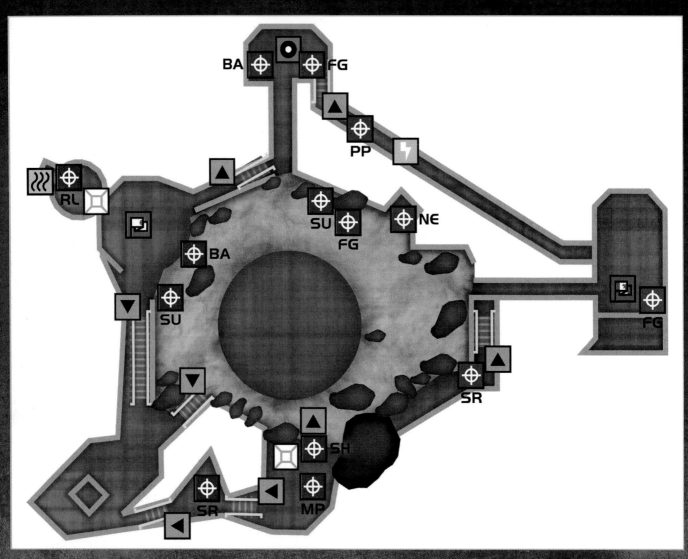

Ascension lower level.

A view from above.

Ascension scenery.

Ascension Weapons

- The lone Banshee can be useful but practice your rolls. Someone with the Rocket Launcher will have a great shot as you try to strafe other players.

- The Rocket Launcher is at the bottom of the Leap of Faith platform. If someone is piloting the Banshee, this is the way to bring him back down to earth. The launcher is also crucial in Juggernaut games.

- Ascension is not very big and it features some tight corridors. If you like close combat, grab the shotgun and stay out of view of the snipers.

- Okay, so it isn't exactly a weapon but it will help you win a battle or two. As mentioned in Chapter 5, Advanced Combat, the Overshield is a great trump card. Listen for the sound of someone else charging. If you hear the sound, don't engage the player coming from the Overshield spot.

- The sniper perch has a great view, but you might find that staying on the dish level with the Battle Rifle will give you more options.

- The dish is one of the best dual Needler killing zones. Just make sure that you have some cover so that you can hide after you have fired off your shards.

The Ascension Banshee attacks.

Ascension Rocket Launcher.

Ascension Shotgun.

The Ascension Overshield.

An Ascension Battle Rifle.

An Ascension Needler.

Ascension Strategy

- The Ascension Banshee has the best backdrop in the game.
- This small sniper perch is great if you have someone watching your back with the Shotgun.
- The Ascension Leap of Faith takes you to the Rocket Launcher.

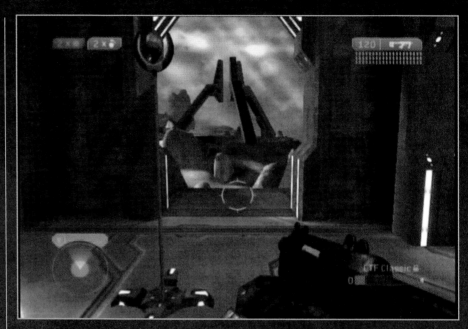

Ascension Red.

Ascension Blue.

Ascension Banshee.

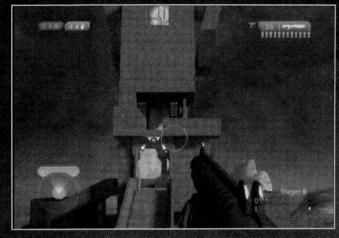

Ascension sniper spot.

Ascension teleporter.

Ascension leap to rockets.

Beaver Creek

Size: Small

Ideal Number of Players: 2–8

Vehicles Supported: None

Targeted Game Types: 1-on-1, Juggernaut, Slayer, Two-Flag CTF

Territories: Blue Base, Red Base, River

Features: Breakable windows provide an entrance into the bases from above.

Default Weapons:

- Magnum Pistol
- SMG
- Shotgun
- Battle Rifle
- Sniper Rifle
- Rocket Launcher
- Fragmentation Grenades
- Plasma Pistol
- Plasma Rifle
- Needler
- Plasma Grenades

Details: Halo 1 fans probably will feel most comfortable in Beaver Creek. It has undergone relatively few changes since its genesis as Battle Creek. In other words, they didn't dig up any Banshees as they did on that other Halo 1 map. Rumor has it that Battle Creek was originally called Beaver Creek but Bungie changed the name shortly before the launch of Halo 1.

> ### Crew 116 Advice: Beaver Creek FFA
>
> If you spawn near the Battle Rifle, Rocket Launcher, or Sniper Rifle, concentrate on the middle; otherwise teleporter camping is the way to go.
>
> —DJ116

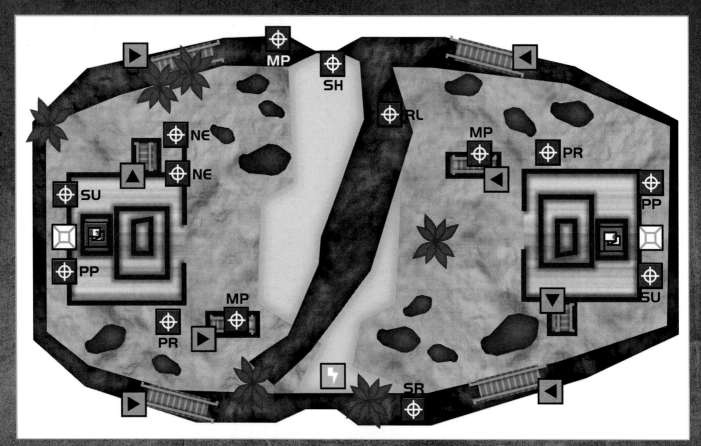

Beaver Creek ground level.

Beaver Creek lower level.

A Beaver Creek teleporter

I don't remember this being here...

Crew 116 Advice: Beaver Creek Map

The ladders up to the Sniper Rifle areas are gone and replaced with ramps. This changes the dynamic in that area a bit, and makes it easier to stop someone going for rockets or the Sniper Rifle. A Shotgun has been added to the map—making up close play more interesting. The Shotgun is even stronger because it's quite near the Overshield.

—*char*

There are a couple of interesting changes since this map was Battle Creek. You can no longer jump out the windows of the red base. This takes away some options for getting in or out of the base. It's easier to get onto the roofs of the bases, both because of wider step up platforms and the Master Chief's super jump.

—*tantrum*

Beaver Creek Weapons

■ The Battle Creek Rocket Launcher was one of the most coveted weapons in Halo 1. In Halo 2, the Beaver Creek version will probably be even more popular. The approach routes to the launcher are easier and the Shotgun will inspire people to go for more one-shot frags.

■ The sniper perches are now accessible via ramps instead of the Battle Creek ladders. For snipers, this means that they are far more vulnerable to grenade tosses. Whereas it used to take an accurate throw to land a grenade in the perch, the angled ramps funnel grenades toward the sniper.

■ The Shotgun is new to these surroundings, and it seems as though it will be a popular choice on this level. Just remember that the Shotgun area will be a grenade magnet. However, if you do get the shottie, you can head to the bases and go for some quick one-shot encounters.

■ The Plasma Pistol is noteworthy because you can DW it with the Magnum for some fast action. Use the overcharge on shields and then use the Magnum to finish off your target.

■ The Magnum offers a headshot bonus so use it when your opponent's shields are down. It is an extremely effective weapon in a shield-less game.

■ The Plasma Rifle provides another shield blasting option. If you aren't a big fan of the Plasma Ball shot, you might want to DW this with the SMG. The Plasma Rifle may not drop shields as fast as the Plasma Ball, but it does allow you to miss a few times. Also, the SMG is better than the Magnum if you aren't sure that your opponent's shields are down.

Crew 116 Advice: Beaver Creek Plasma Pistols

There's one Plasma Pistol outside each porter. This makes the area behind the ports awesome. I would pick up the Plasma Pistol + a human weapon over the Shotgun + Overshield.

—*tantrum*

Beaver Creek Rocket Launcher.

Beaver Creek Sniper Rifle.

Beaver Creek Shotgun.

Beaver Creek Plasma Pistol.

A Beaver Creek Magnum.

Beaver Creek Plasma Rifle.

Beaver Creek Strategy

- The Battle Creek bases have been altered for the Beaver Creek map. There are now two entrances from above and it's easier to get onto the roof.

- The Rocket Launcher spawn spot gives you a great view of the map.

- It is now easier to get up to the Rocket Launcher by running up the angled rock formation.

- The Overshield is in a small cave and a depression. Expect that grenades will find this spot.

- These breakable windows offer a quick entrance into the base. For example, if you have to retreat from the roof, this gives you a well-covered egress option. On the other hand, if you're going for a flag, the windows are an excellent ingress route.

Beaver Creek Red.

Beaver Creek Blue.

Beaver Creek rocket blue view.

Beaver Creek rocket red view.

The Beaver Creek Overshield.

Beaver Creek windows.

Burial Mounds

Size: Medium

Ideal Number of Players: 4-8

Vehicles Supported: Banshee, Ghost, Scorpion, Spectre, Warthogs, Wraith

Targeted Game Types: Assault, CTF, Slayer, Territories

Territories: Base, Boulder Field, Bridge, Generators, Ribs

Features: Stationary turrets

Default Weapons:
Shotgun
Battle Rifle
Sniper Rifle
Rocket Launcher
Fragmentation Grenades
Stationary Turrets
Plasma Pistol
Plasma Rifle
Plasma Sword
Needler
Carbine
Beam Rifle
Plasma Grenades

Details: The layout of Burial Mounds is enough to start any sniper salivating. The combination of its medium size and openness make it ideal for ranged weapons. The map is asymmetrical; in some team games, one side will start in the structure and the other will be in an open space.

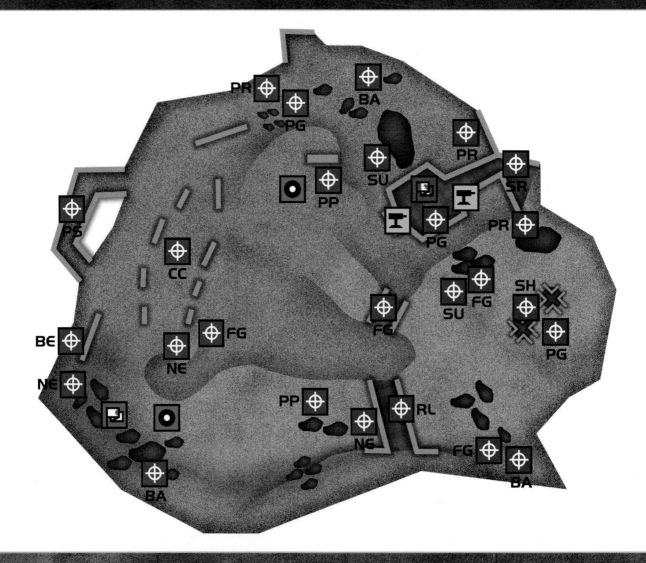

Burial Mounds ground level.

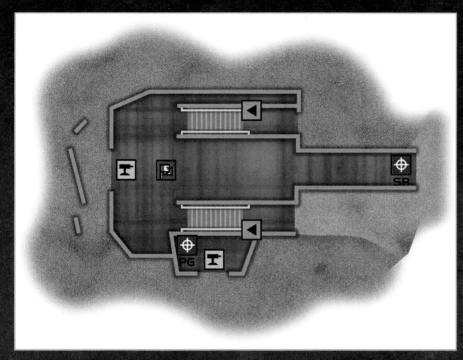

Burial Mounds base level.

Crew 116 Advice: Burial Mounds

This is probably my favorite map. I try to control the map with a few ranged weapons. Unlike Headlong, there are plenty of them. People just seem to take very predictable paths on this map. It's also a moderately sized map, making it conducive to a ranged game.

If you want to survive, learn how to get from base to base without being seen. Play as both sides to see which areas hide the line of sight. This is particularly important for assaulting the base that houses the mini-guns.

Also, learn where the jeep can go and where it can't. Finally, learn how to spawn camp the low base and how to break it. For flag games, camping the lower base is pretty easy.

—*char*

Crew 116 Advice: Burial Mounds FFA

There is a ledge by the rocket location that gives you a great viewpoint to cover people coming from either base. A Battle Rifle and sniper combination can rack up lots of kills.

—*DJ116*

Crew 116 Advice: Burial Mounds

Burial Mounds is interesting because it has sub-areas where fights will occur. There's the skeleton (ribs), the two bases, and the "purple machines" (the batteries outside the high base).

—*tantrum*

Burial Mounds coop.

Burial Mounds highway.

Burial Mounds
Weapons

- If you're caught out in the open, you won't last long against the turrets. You might want to 'bait and switch' the turret by having one player jump out while another picks off the enemy firing the turret. Just make sure that you don't get your whole team in enfilade as you're rushing the base.

- Ghosts obviously allow you to move quickly around the map. In addition, Burial Mounds offers some tight areas where a Ghost can mow down trapped prey.

- If you like ranged weapons, catching people out in the open is great fun. Burial Mounds is well suited to fans of the rifles.

- Find a well-hidden perch and go for the long strike. Whether your team is on offense or defense, you can support them from afar.

- The sword is interesting because the level is so open. People won't expect you to pull out the sword so wait until the right time and use the surprise to your advantage. When someone is chasing you, run behind a rock and switch to this blade. When they come around, you'll have them cold.

- The Rocket Launcher should have clear shots at vehicles. Guard the choke points so that the other team can't support their advance with vehicles.

Burial Mounds Stationary Turrets.

Burial Mounds Ghost.

A Burial Mounds Beam Rifle.

Burial Mounds Sniper Rifle.

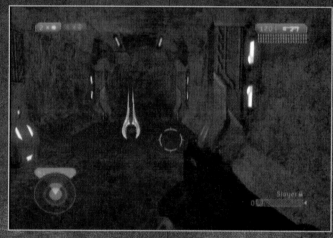

Burial Mounds Sword.

Burial Mounds Rocket Launcher.

Crew 116 Advice: Burial Mounds Base

The turrets on Burial Mounds are destructible. Blowing them with grenades or rockets early in a team game is valuable.

—*tantrum*

Burial Mounds Strategy

- Watch for infantry out in the open and mow them down with the Stationary Turrets.

- The Rocket Launcher location is easily visible to snipers.

- Burial Mounds has some choke points that will give a player with rockets a great shot at vehicles.

- Open layouts, such as Burial Mounds, favor players who are proficient with medium range weapons such as the Battle Rifle and the Covenant Carbine.

Crew 116 Advice: Burial Mounds

Burial Mounds is basically an "uneven" map, so for flag/assault games, they'll usually be single flag. The upper base will be the defense side, and it's pretty defensible. The one interesting trick with the upper base is that you can jump into it in front of the lower turret (there's a little notch in the rock).

—*tantrum*

Burial Mounds Red.

Burial Mounds Blue.

Burial Mounds turrets.

Burial Mounds rockets.

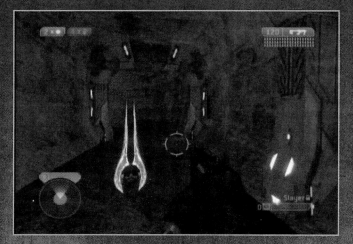

The Burial Mounds sword.

Burial Mounds Battle Rifle.

Coagulation

Size: Large

Ideal Number of Players: 8–16

Vehicles Supported: Banshee, Ghost, Scorpion, Spectre, Warthogs, Wraith

Targeted Game Types: CTF, Assault, Territories, KotH

Territories: Blue Base, Hill, Red Base, Rockslide

Features: Stationary Turrets, Large open space.

Default Weapons:

Magnum Pistol

Shotgun

Battle Rifle

Sniper Rifle

Rocket Launcher

Fragmentation Grenades

Plasma Pistol

Plasma Rifle

Needler

Brute Shot

Plasma Grenades

Details: Fans of Blood Gulch will be happy to see this map. Coagulation is the other map that that was carried forward from the Halo 1 days. However, time has passed and some things have obviously changed. Trees have grown, rockslides have brought down some of the canyon walls, and the bases have been excavated to reveal hidden Banshees.

Coagulation may be based on another map, but the trees and rocks provide more cover for infantry and the extra vehicle option have changed the landscape of strategy on this territory.

Blue team members will be happy to find that the Overshield is not far from their teleporter destination.

A familiar view.

Game on!

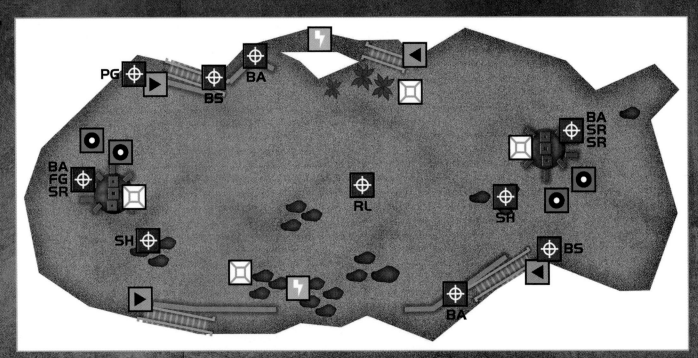

Coagulation ground level.

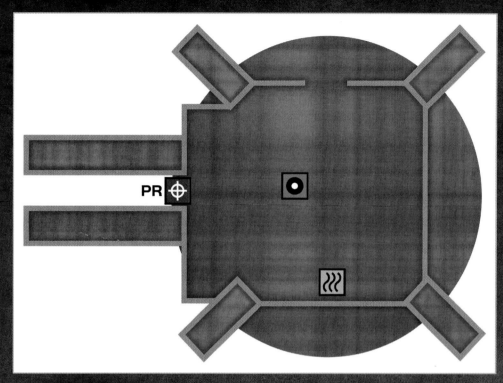

Coagulation base lower level.

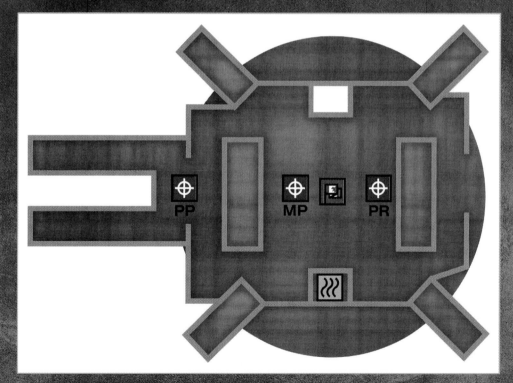

Coagulation base upper level.

Crew 116 Advice: Coagulation

Without many ranged weapons, I suspect this map will be dominated by vehicles. The ports have a ton of cover now, making it harder to hold them against your enemy—and they've also been moved back, which adds to the difficulty. The three level base is kind of neat. I'm curious to see how easy it is to defend and escape.

—char

Coagulation Weapons

- The Banshee is an interesting addition to this new version of Blood Gulch. Remember that you can parachute yourself into the base or other hard to reach locations.

- The Rocket Launcher is now in the middle of the map. On Blood Gulch, it used to be closer to the Overshield cave. In addition, the Rocket Launcher used to have some cover, but now it doesn't. This will make it more difficult to reach the launcher. However, if you are able to get invisible rockets, you can still cause some serious trouble.

- The Sniper Rifle will continue to be an essential weapon on this map. Despite all the new rocks and tress, the rifle spawn location still gives you a view of the other base.

- The Overshield is so close to the blue teleport exit that it seems many people will want to play for the blue team.

- The Brute Shot might be tough to use in the open, but in the caves, it could be useful.

- The Shotgun is a short run from the base. Expect that snipers will watch the Shotgun spawn area.

A Coagulation Banshee.

Coagulation Rocket Launcher.

Coagulation Sniper Rifle.

Coagulation Overshield.

Coagulation Brute Shot.

Coagulation Shotgun.

Coagulation Strategy

- The Coagulation base structures are symmetrical but the environment around them is not.

- The blue teleporter offers a significant shortcut to the Active Camouflage powerup.

- Since its first incarnation, this map has gained a Banshee under each base. Use the Banshee for supporting infantry, reconnaissance, and aerial drops onto locations of your choice.

- The Overshield is in a cave and it's also most useful in the caves.

- Blood Gulch snipers still have excellent vantage points on this map.

- The terrain is more rugged than Blood Gulch so you'll have to learn to avoid more obstacles.

Coagulation Red base.

Coagulation sniper perch.

A Coagulation Banshee.

Coagulation Overshield.

Coagulation sniper perch.

A Warthog on Coagulation.

Colossus

Size: Large

Ideal Number of Players: 8–16

Vehicles Supported: None

Targeted Game Types: Assault, CTF, Slayer

Territories: Blue Base, Command Deck, Red Base, Trench

Features: Very well designed factory-style conveyor system. Bridge across the middle is removed for some game types. Gravity lift that carries players up to the sniper spot.

Crew 116 Advice: The Colossus Map

Don't fall through the holes in the floor at the end of the conveyors on the bottom level. There is an interesting strategy for ball games; if you have the ball and can keep jumping into the lift, you can avoid getting killed for a few seconds—it's hard to hit someone in the lift.

—*tantrum*

Default Weapons:

Magnum Pistol

Shotgun

Battle Rifle

Fragmentation Grenades

Plasma Pistol

Plasma Rifle

Needler

Beam Rifle

Plasma Grenades

Details: This level must have required considerable work. The level is a factory setting with lots of moving parts.

In FFA, the area of the map where the lift lands people is a great place to hang out with a ranged weapon and a short range weapon—for example, the Battle Rifle with the Shotgun or the Battle Rifle and a Plasma Pistol/SMG combination. This is a high traffic area so there is lots of action.

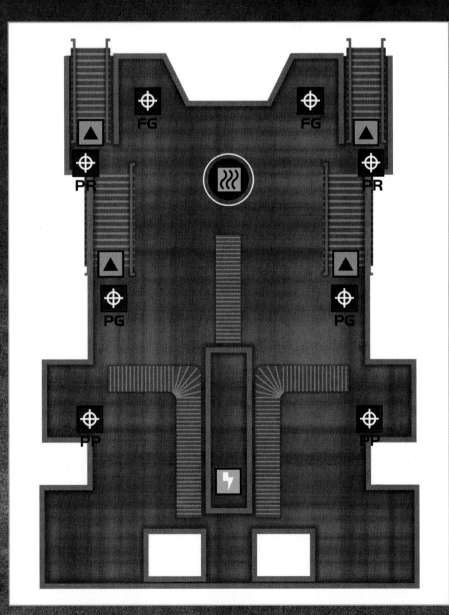

Colossus main level.

The view from below.

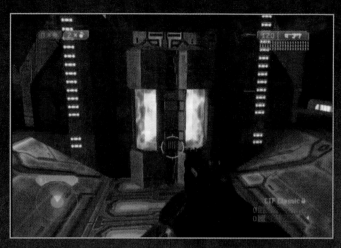

Taking a ride.

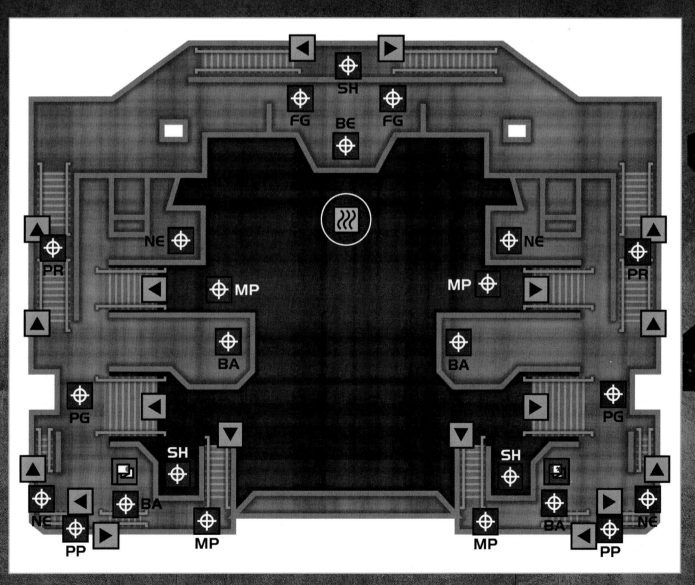

Colossus upper level.

Colossus Weapons

- The Beam Rifle appears to be the center piece weapon on this map. Whether you use the large gravity lift or the ramps leading up through the tower, you will come out in the Beam Rifle spawn location. For this reason, the best practice might be to grab the rifle and then find a more defensible sniper perch.

- The Shotgun will be useful but try not to get caught running around with it in the middle of the map.

- Dual Plasma Rifles could be fun, but just remember that in this dark map you'll be lit up like a firecracker.

- As always, DW the Magnum with an overcharged Plasma Pistol. Check the carnage report to see if you are scoring headshots with the Magnum.

- The open Colossus area is a nice size for DW Needlers.

- People running across the middle will be good marks for the Battle Rifle.

The Colossus Beam Rifle.

A Colossus Shotgun.

A Colossus Plasma Rifle.

A Colossus Magnum.

A Colossus Needler.

A Colossus Battle Rifle.

Colossus Strategy

- The Colossus bases are symmetrical. Learn the jumps so that you can get around the map quickly.
- The bridge between the bases is removed for some game types. For example, you wouldn't want the bridge there for CTF.
- Use the large gravity lift as a shortcut to the Beam Rifle.
- The treadmill is a nice touch.
- If you find a player next to a glowing container, make him pay.
- The Beam Rifle offers a definite advantage on this map.

Colossus Red.

Colossus Blue.

Colossus lift.

Inside the treadmill.

Use the environment.

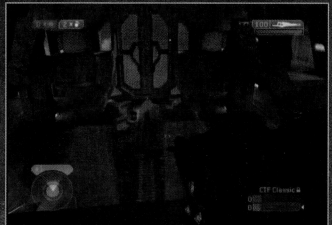

The Beam Rifle.

Headlong

Size: Medium

Ideal Number of Players: 8–16

Vehicles Supported: Banshee, Ghost, Warthogs

Targeted Game Types: Assault, CTF, Slayer

Territories: Alley, Building Site, Corner Building, Construction Pit, Gate Bridge, Statue

Features: Ocean view, stationary guns

Default Weapons:

Magnum Pistol

SMG

Shotgun

Battle Rifle

Sniper Rifle

Rocket Launcher Fragmentation Grenades

Stationary Turrets

Plasma Pistol

Plasma Rifle

Plasma Sword

Needler

Carbine

Brute Shot

Details: This seaside level offers some Halo 2 urban warfare. Use the vehicles to get around quickly—you will be surprised how many places you can go with the vehicles. However, note that the paths are extremely predictable.

Crew 116 Advice: Headlong

This is a neat map—it will probably be the new Gulch. There are limited ranged weapon options. Also, there are good routes around the map with a reasonable center area for vehicles. This is another example of a great asymmetric map.

—char

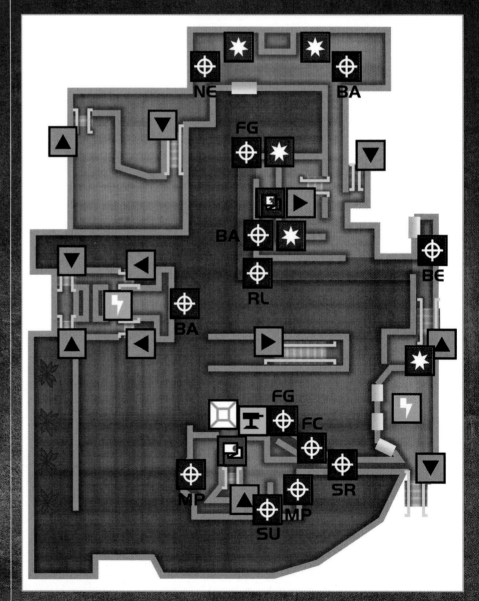

Headlong upper level.

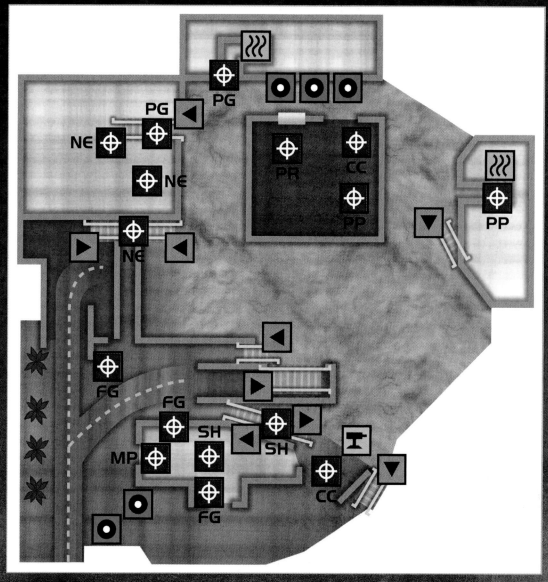

Headlong ground level.

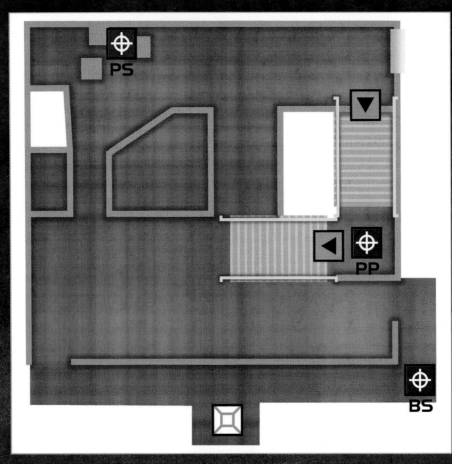

Headlong tower level

Vehicles can go to many places.

Looking over Headlong.

Headlong Weapons

- Headlong features enough vehicles that the Rocket Launcher could be a key factor on this map. Make sure you lock on before you fire your rockets because you won't be able to get much ammunition.

- The vehicles deserve mention as effective weapons on this map. The Ghost is nice and maneuverable so it would be a good choice for FFA games. However, in a team match-up, a pair in a Warthog could rip through an opposing team.

- The Brute Shot could be great in the Headlong structures. Bounce some rounds around corners to get the campers.

- The Plasma Sword will be great for the buildings but don't use it in the open areas. A sniper would like nothing better than to cut down someone carrying this blade.

- There are numerous nooks and crannies that a Headlong sniper could use.

- The Plasma Carbine could be used in some of the open spaces, but I wouldn't try it in the buildings.

Headlong Rocket Launcher.

Some Headlong Vehicles.

Headlong Brute Shot.

Headlong Sword.

Headlong Sniper Rifle.

Headlong Carbine.

Headlong Strategy

- The Active Camouflage powerup will help you move about the map freely.
- There are many vehicles on this map. Drive them around and you'll find the best routes to take.
- Jump up on this bus to get to the Overshield from the street.

Crew 116 Advice: Headlong Bases

This is another unbalanced map. I think getting the flag out of the bottom base is harder than getting the flag out of the top base. Although, throwing it out the window next to the flag post is definitely the way to go for that. If you do that and there's a hog at the bottom ready to pick up, it's all over.

—*tantrum*

Crew 116 Advice: The Headlong Active Camouflage

The active cammo is directly on the way to the enemy base. Best to get invis + shotgun, and go straight to the base.

—*tantrum*

Headlong Red.

Headlong Blue.

Headlong teleporter.

Headlong invis.

Headlong vehicles.

Using the bus to get to the Overshield.

Ivory Tower

Size: Small

Ideal Number of Players: 4–8

Vehicles Supported: None

Targeted Game Types: 1-on-1, Assault, CTF, Slayer

Territories: Air Lifts, Crossroads, Elevator, Tunnel, Walkway

Features: Air vents can used to elevate players.

Default Weapons:

- Magnum Pistol
- SMG
- Shotgun
- Battle Rifle
- Sniper Rifle
- Rocket Launcher
- Fragmentation Grenades
- Plasma Pistol
- Plasma Rifle
- Plasma Sword
- Needler
- Carbine
- Plasma Grenades

Details: An intimate level that features a tranquil courtyard. If you get frustrated during a game, you can take it out on a bench in the courtyard or the coconuts in the trees.

The Shotgun often rules this level but a Plasma Pistol and human weapon combination can also work. The sword is useful but some areas have enough space that a player with the shottie can evade a sword fighter long enough to get in a fatal blast.

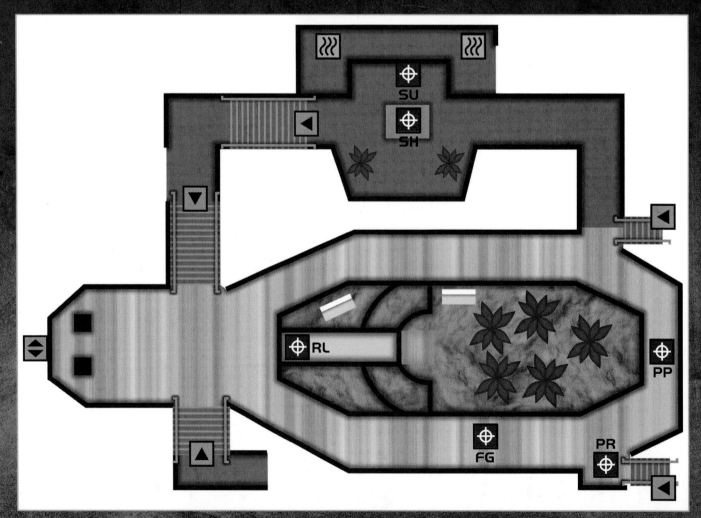

Ivory Tower wooden level.

The Rocket Launcher is surprisingly close to the rockets. Expect to see a lot of the Rocket Launcher defense on this level. If you are the one carrying the Rocket Launcher, be careful firing rockets when you're among the trees in the courtyard—the trees won't go down, but you will.

The top of the elevator is a popular camping spot, and it's also a popular spot for melees. It's common to come upon traffic in this area.

Crew 116 Advice: Ivory Tower Top Level

I think this is the most important area of the map. You're high, have sniper, Plasma Pistol, Overshield, and Shotgun accessible. You can stay at one end of this hallway slaying close up stuff with the Shotgun or plasma, and snipe down the hallway the other way if anyone comes at you. It's uber.

—*tantrum*

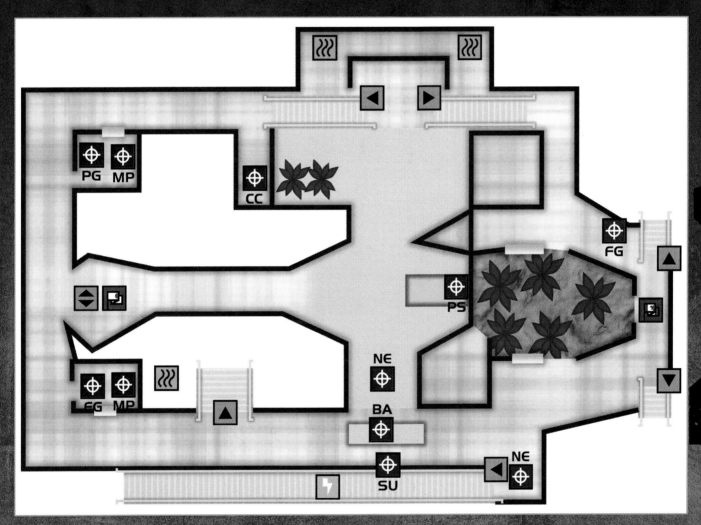

Ivory Tower basement level.

Crew 116 Advice: Ivory Tower

Learn the paths people take through this map. Some areas are high traffic and some aren't. You'll find fights easier if you know where to look. It's easy to run away on this map if a fight goes sour.

—char

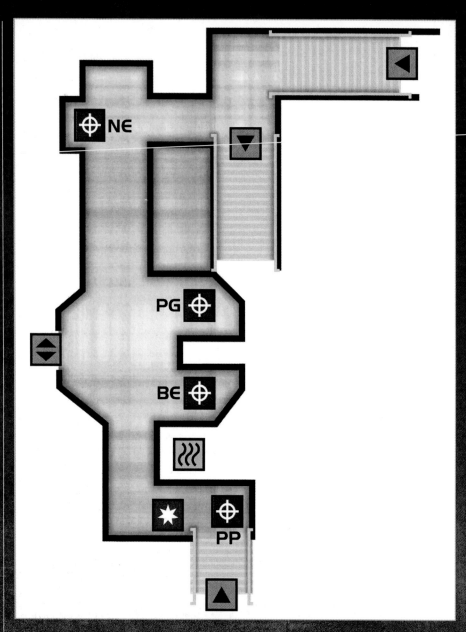

Ivory Tower top level.

Crew 116 Advice: Ivory Tower FFA

Any FFA with six or more people will favor the Shotgun because you will always be in close up battles. Smaller FFA games favor ranged weapons. In these games, the Battle Rifle and Carbine are the keys to the map.

Base games, like CTF and assault, favor ranged weapons because you know where your enemies will be. The Carbine is more accurate at long distances, but is less powerful. Ivory Tower is small enough that Battle Rifle is usually a better choice than Carbine. On maps like Burial Mounds or Waterworks, I prefer the Carbine.

When I do have the Carbine, I like to stay near the double air jumps. You can setup far enough away from the action to have an easy time picking people off from a distance.

—DJ116

The Ivory Tower elevator.

The Ivory Tower park benches.

Ivory Tower Weapons

- The Rocket Launcher is so attractive that people will randomly throw a grenade onto its spawn spot just in case someone happens to be there. If you get the launcher in a team game, take a buddy up to the top level. Your friend can watch your back while you destroy anyone who tries to take the tower.

- Good sword fighters can dominate Ivory Tower. There are enough small spaces that you can run around with it out all the time—just make sure that you pick a good route. The counter to the sword is to learn the map and learn the map and learn the map. If you can run around the map backwards, you will be able to retreat from a sword while you spray your foe.

- This Overshield is on a ramp leading to the tower. If you happen to be running up that way, finding this powerup on the ground is serendipitous.

- The Shotgun is extremely effective and the most versatile of the power weapons on Ivory Tower. The location has a number of approach angles so it's hard to camp. However, even if you use the air vents, some players will be able to tag you.

- The Sniper Rifle is great for supporting your team's push to the courtyard base.

- The Ivory Tower Covenant Carbine is probably the best-hidden weapon in the game. Use it to pick off people in the open courtyard space.

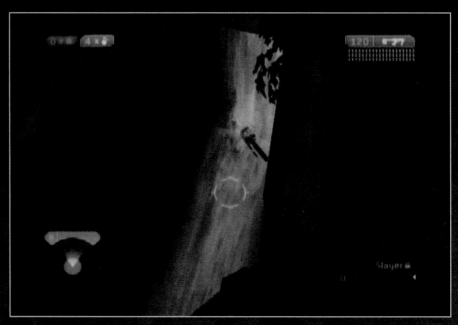

The Ivory Tower Rocket Launcher.

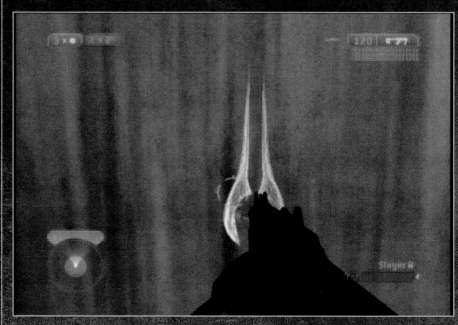

The Ivory Tower Sword.

The Ivory Tower Overshield.

The Ivory Tower air vent Shotgun.

The Ivory Tower Sniper Rifle.

The Ivory Tower Carbine.

Note

I was once backing away from a sword on the lower level of Ivory Tower and I thought that I had him. However, I happened to back into a pillar and before I could recover, I was carved up. If I really could run around the map backwards, I may have survived the fight.

Crew 116 Advice: Ivory Tower Shotgun Location

Rockets own this spot. When they see you vent, they'll shoot the wall or where you're landing.

—*tantrum*

Ivory Tower Strategy

- If you're a big fan of long-range weapons, this probably isn't the right map for you. Most of the fighting is tight and hectic.

- The Ivory Tower red base is located next to the courtyard. In team games, defending this base is exciting because attacks can come from so many different directions. Some teams will split up to attack from each side and through the courtyard.

- The blue base is located in the basement. Use short-range weapons when you are in this area.

- These air vents give you a shortcut to the Shotgun.

- The Rocket Launcher mounts an effective rocket defense.

- The top of Ivory Tower attracts many players during FFA games. Figure out how to get frags without being assaulted from almost all sides.

- The flower beds are accessible via an unaided jump from the wooden platform. However, you have to first jump to the ledge that angles up to the planter.

Ivory Tower Red.

Ivory Tower Blue.

Ivory Tower air vents.

The Ivory Tower Rocket Launcher location.

Covering the top ramp and the Shotgun.

An Ivory Tower flower bed.

Lockout

Size: Small

Ideal Number of Players: 2–8

Vehicles Supported: Banshee

Targeted Game Types: 1-on-1, Assault, CTF, Slayer

Territories: Center Room, Cliff Room, Lift, Roof, Walkway

Features: Lots of drop-offs

Default Weapons:

Magnum Pistol

SMG

Shotgun

Battle Rifle

Sniper Rifle

Rocket Launcher

Fragmentation Grenades

Plasma Pistol

Plasma Rifle

Plasma Sword

Needler

Plasma Grenades

Details: This a small map with lots of sword-friendly tight corridors. Lockout is an installation on the side of a massive cliff. Around the installation is a snowy blue sky and below is a misty drop-off. Most of the level is in shades of blue.

This map essentially has three levels: the lower level, the courtyard, and the upper (tower) level. If you are playing a team game, one team will start on top of a high platform and the other team will start across the map in the lowest room.

Some people refer to the spot below the sniper perch as the 'ledge of invincibility.' It provides a full view of the courtyard and nearby attackers will appear on your radar—or in your reticle.

This map is one of the few levels that is the right size for the Needler. Try DW Needlers while you watch the open courtyard area. If you stay in the more cramped lower parts of this level, then the Plasma Sword can be very effective.

There are hidden ledges on the sides of many of the catwalks that make for good perches and ambush spots. Some people have managed to jump onto some of the cables that run between different areas of the level. If you can do this regularly, it might make for a cool escape route or sniping perch.

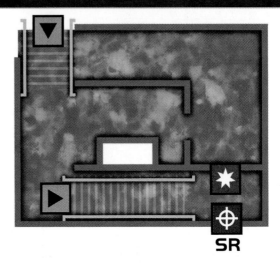

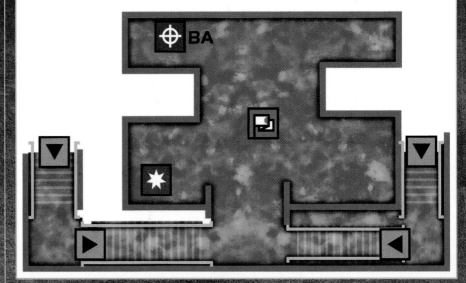

Lockout tower level.

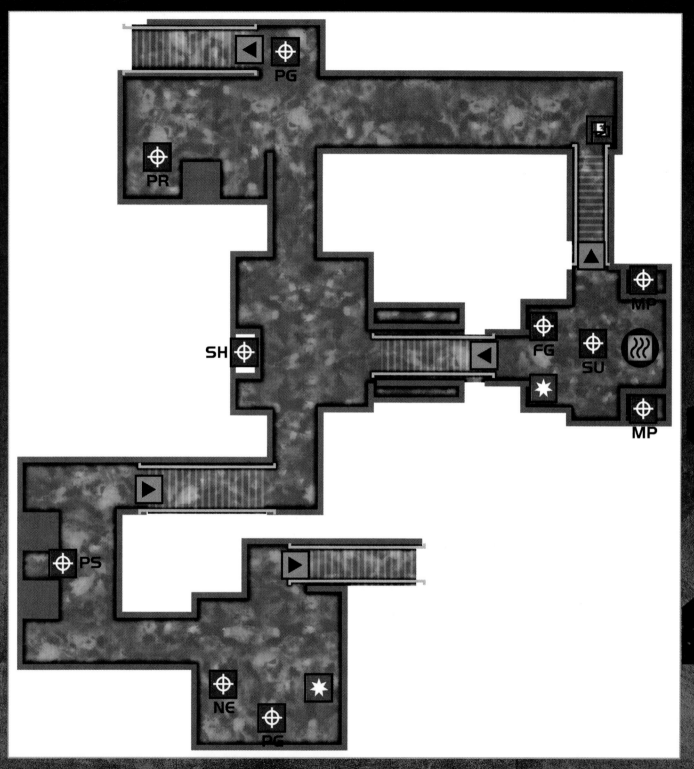

Lockout lower level.

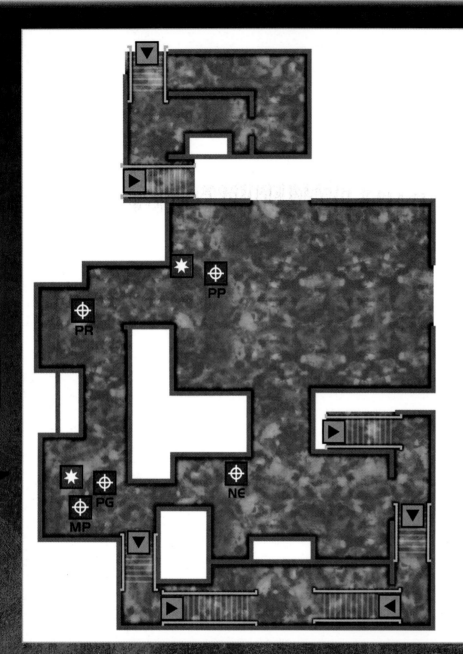

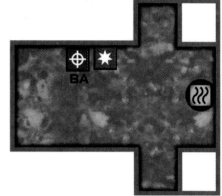

Lockout courtyard level.

Crew 116 Advice: Lockout

Know your way around the map. You can get from one part of the map to another really fast if you know the right way to go. Learn the trick jumps; there are a bunch of them. Many jumps allow you to change levels without much risk of falling to your death.

—char

Crew 116 Advice: Lockout

The sword rules Lockout.

—char

Crew 116 Advice: Lockout FFA

Sniper location is the best location to get kills. Bring a Battle Rifle here and own the entire top of the board, or bring a Shotgun/Sword here and rack up frags below.

—DJ116

Lockout courtyard jump—grenade optional.

The first one to go for the lower Battle Rifle.

Lockout Weapons

- Having the Plasma Sword will allow you to rule with an iron fist.

- The Sniper Rifle is located on the high tower. However, the exploding containers and grenades make the high perch undesirable. Grab the rifle and then run down one level to the 'ledge of invincibility.' From there you can snipe the tower base, the gravity lift, and the lower base. If someone approaches from underneath, he will appear on your radar. Simply watch him start up the ramp and drop in on him.

- If you want to get at someone on this ledge, jump from the courtyard side onto the ramp that leads up to the Sniper Rifle spawn spot.

- There are plenty of exploding containers on the Lockout level. Use them to take out players who forget to stay away from them.

- DW with Needlers on Lockout is a blast. Stay near cover while pincushioning players running across the courtyard.

- For some precision work, use Plasma Grenades to drop shields and then headshot your marks with the Magnum.

- For a little fun, try shooting the exploding containers and then firing at the bits in the air. It's like Halo 2 skeet shooting.

The Lockout Plasma Sword location.

The Lockout Sniper Rifle.

Some Lockout powder kegs.

Lockout Needler.

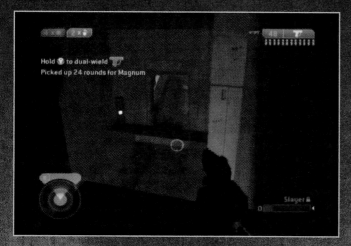

Lockout Magnum.

A Lockout Battle Rifle.

Lockout Strategy

- The Red base is located on the lower level. One issue with this location is that there are a couple of places where an opposing team can cover most of the exits from the base. If you're taking sniper fire, use the ramp that leads to the room under the courtyard.

- A definite advantage of this base is that you can easily take a flag from the Blue base to the Red spot. Grab the flag, jump down to the courtyard, run across the courtyard, and use the corner to jump down to the ramp above the Red flag spot. Just don't die while you are in the air—the flag will likely drop off the map and you'll have to wait for it to re-spawn.

- An effective technique is to grab the Sniper Rifle and take it to the Blue base. From the top, you can snipe people approaching from many directions and you can prevent the other team from using the sniper perch against you.

- The Plasma Sword is often the weapon of choice on the Lockout map. Grab the sword and run around the lower part of the map. If you go to the courtyard, you will likely be outnumbered or get picked off by a rifle.

- The Shotgun is also effective in the tight sections of Lockout. Many players will choose to camp on the angled Lockout walls and ambush players who run and gun. If you want to counter this tactic, throw a grenade into the room before you enter.

Lockout Red.

Lockout Blue.

- Stay out of the courtyard if you want to do well on this map. The exceptions to this rule are when you feel that you can quickly get more than one frag by joining into the chaos or when you are dead set to get the Plasma Pistol.

- The ledge below the Sniper Rifle is a strong position.

Crew 116 Advice: Lockout Blue Base

You can jump up onto the base using that sloped face. It's tricky, but totally deadly for assault.

—tantrum

Crew 116 Advice: Lockout Shotgun

The Shotgun is great, but it's out of the way. You have to spend a lot of time getting it, and during that time you could be pwning folks.

—tantrum

The Lockout Sword.

The Lockout Shotgun.

Lockout Courtyard.

Lockout lower sniper perch.

Midship

Size: Small

Ideal Number of Players: 4-8

Vehicles Supported: None

Targeted Game Types: 1-on-1, Assault, CTF, Slayer

Territories: Batteries, Center, Moonside Deck, Planetside Deck, Walkway

Features: Gravity lifts, teeter-totter platform, debris floating outside the windows.

Default Weapons:

Shotgun

Battle Rifle

Fragmentation Grenades

Plasma Pistol

Plasma Rifle

Plasma Sword

Needler

Carbine

Plasma Grenades

Details: This is a small dark map with a relatively simple layout. Many dual Plasma Rifle battles happen on this map.

Crew 116 Advice: Midship

This map is almost all Covenant weapons—get good with the Plasma Rifle. The map is simple. Just keep an eye out for where the action is happening. You basically can see the entire map.

—*char*

There are gravity lifts below the bases; they're a really fast way to get around. In addition, there are small ledges above many of the doorways that allow people to sit and wait for victims to walk through, then drop in behind them and deliver a surprise.

The center gets busy.

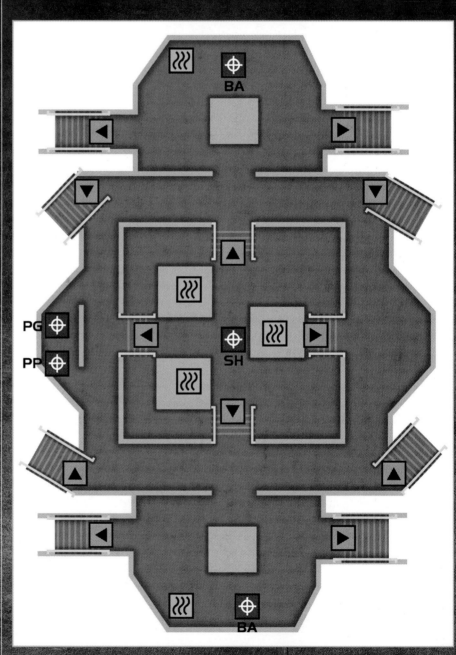

Midship main level.

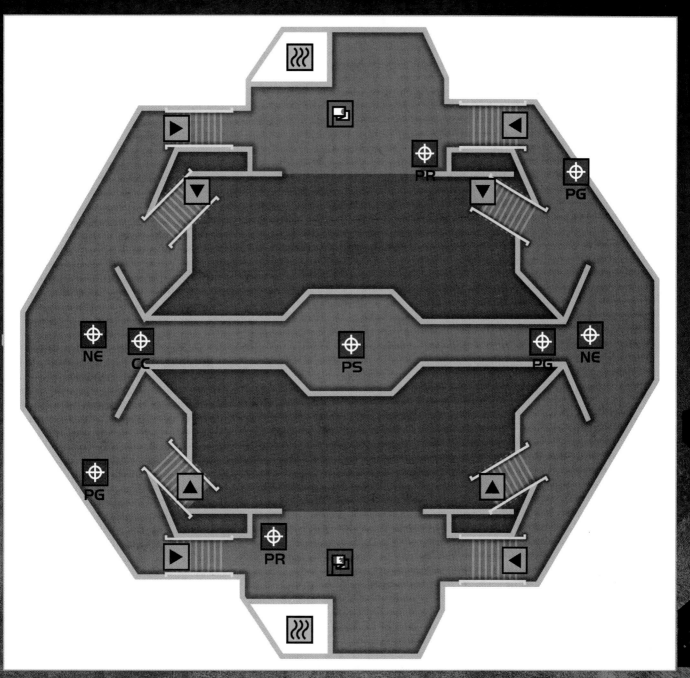

Midship platform level.

Midship Weapons

- The Plasma Sword can be either the ultimate base defense or base assault weapon.

- The Shotgun is the other weapon to use in the Midship bases. Having the Shotgun and the Battle Rifle can give you more options than most combinations on the map.

- A defender with DW Needlers can light up attackers and then hold them off with grenades.

- Of all the Halo 2 levels, it seems clear that Midship will be the one with the most plasma stick frags.

- Since Midship is dark, DW Plasma Rifles is a good light show. Remember that these rifles have a bit of a spread.

- The Carbine is useful for poaching players in the opposite base.

The Midship Plasma Sword.

The Midship Shotgun.

A Midship Needler.

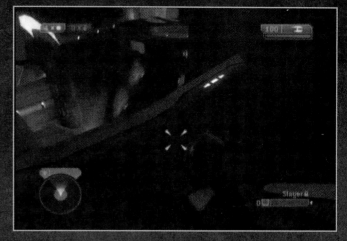

Some Midship Plasma Grenades.

A Midship Plasma Rifle.

The Midship Carbine.

Midship Strategy

- The Midship bases are symmetrical and within clear view of one another.

- When guarding the base, consider all of the ingress options: two ramps up the sides, the gravity lift, and a jump from the upper platform.

- The gravity lifts offer a convenient entrance into the Midship bases. In FFA games, they all also a great way to 'add' into battles.

- If you're playing defense, taking out enemies across the Midship map is one of the most enjoyable precision shots. While still in your own base, you can support your offense by taking pot shots at the other base.

- This perch gives you a decent view of half of the map.

- If you're looking for some fun on Midship, use the middle gravity lifts to get up on the short pillars surrounding the Shotgun. You won't be able to stay there long, but players will be surprised to see you there.

Midship Red.

Midship Blue.

A Midship gravity lift.

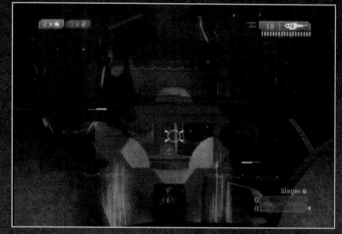

The view across Midship.

Up on top...

Midship middle lift.

Waterworks

Size: Large

Ideal Number of Players: 8–16

Vehicles Supported: All

Targeted Game Types: Assault, CTF, Territories

The Waterworks drop-off.

Territories: Blue Base, Blue Bridge, Center Bridge, Red Base, Red Bridge

Features: Stalactites can be shot down.

Default Weapons:

Magnum Pistol

SMG

Shotgun

Battle Rifle

Sniper Rifle

Rocket Launcher

Fragmentation Grenades

Stationary Turrets

Plasma Pistol

Plasma Sword

Needler

Carbine

Beam Rifle

Brute Shot

Plasma Grenades

Details: Waterworks is a large map with varying degrees of light. The map is inside a cavern that features an enormous plant and stalactites hanging from the ceiling. Most battles on this map will involve vehicles or ranged weapons. However, once you're in the middle structure or a base, the Plasma Sword would be useful.

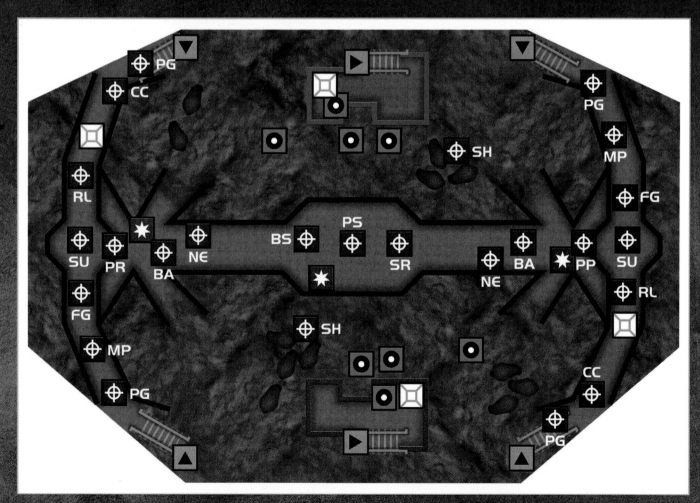

Waterworks Ground Level.

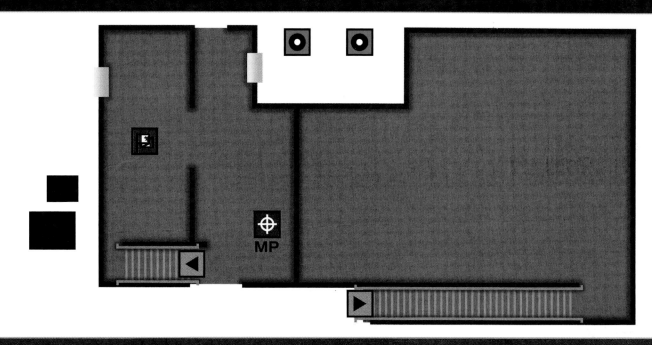

Waterworks Base Ground Level.

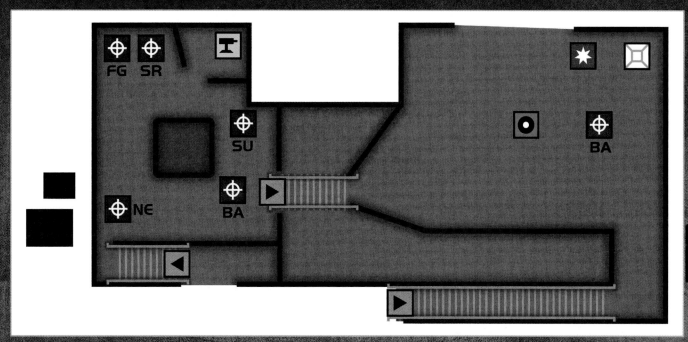

Waterworks Base Top Level.

Waterworks Weapons

- The powerhouse on Waterworks is the Wraith. If your team is able to secure both heavy vehicles, you use them to lockdown the other base.

- The Banshee is a great way to move around and counter the heavy vehicle attack. Shoot down the stalactites so that they land on enemy vehicles and players.

- The Rocket Launcher is enough to make any pilot think twice about leaving the ground.

- The Sniper Rifle is certainly useful but the contrails seem to be even more visible on this map.

- The turrets can take out any infantry that gets too close to your base. A Wraith or Scorpion easily silence the turret.

- The Brute Shot is in the middle area opposite the Sniper Rifle. Use it in the Forerunner structures.

A Waterworks Wraith.

A Waterworks Banshee.

Crew 116 Advice: Waterworks

I think this map will be the new Sidewinder. The areas in front of the base are big, open, killing fields. There are very limited paths through the map. Vehicles are key to this map. Learn them, and use them for offense and defense—particularly the Wraith tank.

—*char*

The Waterworks Rocket Launcher.

A Waterworks Sniper Rifle.

A Waterworks Stationary Turret.

The Waterworks Brute Shot.

Waterworks Strategy

- The Waterworks bases are virtually symmetrical.
- Use the heavy vehicles to lockdown the other team's base.
- The teleporter offers a shortcut to the Rocket Launcher. Grab it and save it for enemy Banshees.
- The open spaces in front of each base are the most dangerous areas on the map. Stay away from them unless you have a specific plan in mind.
- Few sniper perches give you such a view.
- The vehicles spawn right next to each base. If you can steal the other team's vehicles, you can dominate.

Crew 116 Advice: Waterworks Strategy

An interesting strategy is to control the big tower in the middle. Another strategy is just to drive around it. I think the latter is more effective.

There's a back ramp up into the bases, and a box on the side of the base that you can use to jump in. No need to go in through the front or back doors if they're guarded.

—*tantrum*

Waterworks Red.

Waterworks Blue.

Waterworks teleporter.

Open areas in front of the bases are killing fields.

Waterworks middle sniper.

Waterworks vehicles.

Zanzibar

Size: Medium

Ideal Number of Players: 6–16

Vehicles Supported: Ghost, Warthog, Wraith

Targeted Game Types: Assault, CTF, Slayer (snipers), Territories

Territories: Base, Camp Froman, Control Tower, Gate, Sea Wall

Features: Base gate can be manually opened; ramp to wheel structure can be lowered manually.

Zanzibar Wheel.

Default Weapons:

SMG

Shotgun

Battle Rifle

Sniper Rifle

Rocket Launcher

Fragmentation Grenades

Stationary Turrets

Plasma Rifle

Plasma Sword

Needler

Plasma Grenades

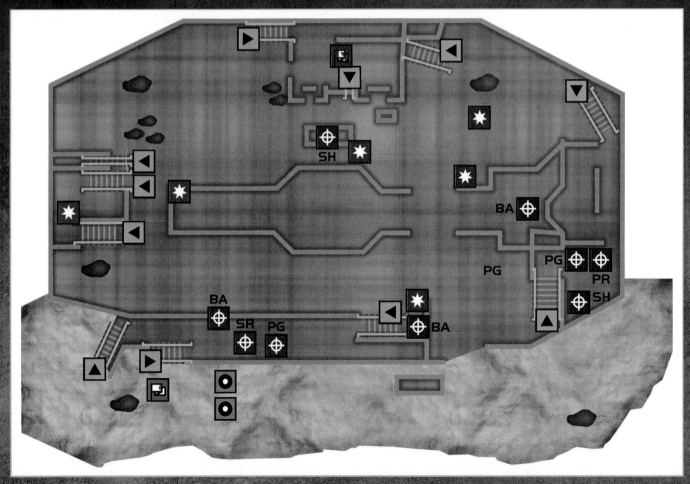

Zanzibar Ground Level.

Details: Zanzibar was the one map that most Halo fans had seen before Halo 2 was released. The map is relatively large and is primarily outside. The main feature of Zanzibar is a gigantic wheel that is constantly spinning and offering rides to players. However, there are plenty of other interesting elements in this map. For example, one of the bases is on the Zanzibar beach. Those brave enough to venture into the water will find No Swimming signs that warn of sharks in the area.

Crew 116 Advice: Zanzibar

Grab the Battle Rifle and Shotgun and clean up. Rockets aren't really worth going out of the way for FFA, since the snipers won't let you get far.

—*DJ116*

Figure out when it's appropriate to use the jeep. It's not always a bright idea to start a CTF or Assault game with a jeep run.

This map has some trick jumps and optimal routes for getting places. Learn how to get around the map fast. Learn all the ways into the base and use them during assaults.

—*char*

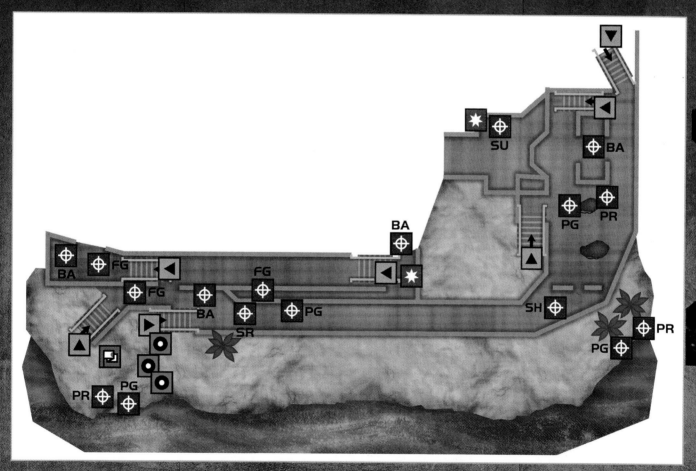

Zanzibar Sea Wall Level.

Itiplayer Maps

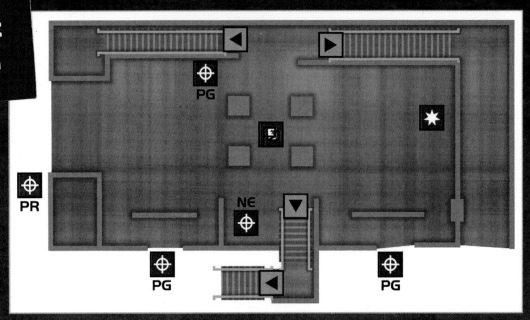

Zanzibar Base Ground Level.

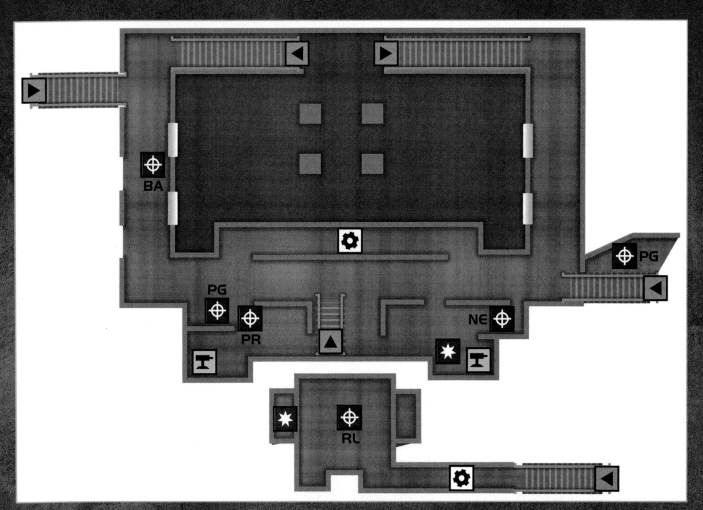

Zanzibar Base Top Level.

Zanzibar Weapons

- The Zanzibar Rocket Launcher is commonly used for the rocket defense. If you find that you're playing against the Rocket Defense, try to keep the other team honest by loading the flag carrier into a Warthog.

- The Plasma Sword takes some effort to retrieve so many players simply forget about it and hope that they find it on the ground at some point. However, a well-placed grenade will blow the sword out of its hiding spot and onto the bottom of the wheel.

- Camp Froman is a highly contested area of the map. A strong midfield player can cause a tremendous amount of damage from this location.

- The Stationary Turrets are tough to use at the beginning of a round because the team coming from the wall side will usually have a sniper checking for players at the turrets. However, if someone grabs the flag from the base, these guns are a great way to stop them.

- The Shotguns are useful in the base on the wall and in the wheel structure. Generally, you don't want to be out in the open with one of them—other players will take you out with ranged weapons.

- The Battle Rifle is a great choice for covering the Zanzibar open spaces. For example, covering the back of a sniper at Camp Froman. Attacking players will usually come from the open areas when they try to attack. However, the smarter players will use the wheel as cover and only give you a few shots before they are on the Camp Froman ramps.

The Zanzibar Rocket Launcher.

Grabbing the Zanzibar Plasma Sword with a grenade toss.

Zanzibar's 'Camp Froman' Sniper Rifle.

A Zanzibar Stationary Turret.

A Zanzibar Shotgun.

A Zanzibar Battle Rifle.

Zanzibar Strategy

- The Zanzibar Blue base is open beach-side property.

- The Sniper Rifle can be used both offensively and defensively. Generally, teams attacking the base expect to meet a Battle Rifle. If you can get a Sniper Rifle back to the base, you will surprise some folks.

- There are plenty of vehicles on this map and not many routes for them to follow. In team games, use the Rocket Launcher to take out the Puma so that the other team can't use it to transport the flag.

- The Plasma Sword is a great way to defend the Zanzibar base. If you're playing a team game, use the sword to ambush players sneaking into the base.

- Opening the gate will only benefit the team attacking the Zanzibar base. If you're defending the base, you might want to guard the console so that it can't be hacked. If you're playing offense against the base, open the gate so that you can drive a Warthog right up to the flag spot.

- Camp Froman offers an excellent view of both sides of the wheel. Having a player on this ledge is not only great for midfield work but also for reconnaissance.

- The wheel is the most dramatic mechanism in the Halo 2 multiplayer maps. Use the spokes to get up on top of the structure. Once up there, you can go for the Plasma Sword, the Rocket Launcher, or attack the base from the top level. Most people don't expect attackers to enter the base from above.

Crew 116 Advice: Zanzibar Base

Generally, the best way to defend the Zanzibar base is to camp, camp, camp inside it. (It's unfortunate, IMO, but that's probably not relevant.) In assault games, stay close to the base.

—tantrum

Zanzibar Red.

Zanzibar Blue.

A Zanzibar Sniper Rifle.

Zanzibar Vehicles.

Sword on Zanzibar.

The Zanzibar Gate.

The Camp Froman sign.

Riding the Zanzibar wheel.

The MrJukes' Guide to Trick Jumps

Remember that you can gain an extra foot or two by crouching when you jump. If you are going for distance rather than height, you should obviously wait until you are just about to hit the edge before you crouch. I generally refer to that as trying to "catch the edge" with the left thumbstick push. It is necessary to make the Rocket Launcher jump on Zanzibar, for instance.

I almost always crouch jump, even if I'm just clearing something that is waist-high. (I'm sure I'm going to wear my controller out real quick.)

Note that the only jumps that require grenades are the ones that specify that it is an aided jump. The number in parentheses is the difficulty of the jump (1 = Easy, 5 = Hard).

Ascension

Jump up from Overshield gangway to the spiral ramp by the red base then jump up to the base (1).

Jump from red base to the Sniper Rifle below (3—this is a falling danger).

Beaver Creek

Jump off the Sniper Rifle ramp onto a rock and then up to the blue base (2).

Jump off the Magnum ramp onto a ledge and then up to the red base (2).

Grenade jump off the rocket spot onto the blue base (4).

Burial Mounds

Jump into the red tower using the ledge in front. Aim for the notch in the rocks (3).

Coagulation

It's possible to crouch jump onto the top of the base. It's always a good thing to have multiple ways to reach a destination (4).

Colossus

Use the gravity lift to get to the Battle Rifle platform (2).

Jump from the ramp up to area under the Battle Rifle platform (a simple shortcut up the ramp) (1).

Crouch jump from the adjacent platform to the Battle Rifle platform (4).

Jump from a column to the platform (2).

Jump up the small hole in the floor (where containers drop) that leads to the Beam Rifle level (3).

Jump up through the window to get to the Beam Rifle level (2).

Jump up from ramp (next to lift) to the platform below the window (1).

Ivory Tower

Jump into a palm tree by the Shotgun. You can stand on top of them, and they are good for hiding (4—it's hard to stick the landing).

Jump onto the Shotgun platform (1).

Crouch jump from Shotgun platform to hardwood (3).

Jump from Shotgun platform to planter to hardwood (2).

Jump from wooden floor onto ledge and then onto flowerpots near the red base. This is a good shortcut to get from low to high (2).

Jump from the planter next to stairs to a ledge next to the Overshield ramp (then onto ramp). This is an alternative to the air vent that gets you up the ramp (4).

Grenade jump from planter to ledge above the Overshield ramp. This is not very useful (5).

Headlong

You can jump from the Brute Shot platform across to the platform one level down that leads to the base. It's a nice little shortcut (3).

Lockout

Use the curved walls to jump up the front of the blue base (1).

Jump from the Battle Rifle (by the lift) to the lower ramp below the red base (4).

Jump from courtyard to lower ramp (great to bypass defense but then you are surrounded). This allows for a fast cap for the red team (3).

Jump off outside edge of the red flag ramp to the ramp that leads to the sniper tower (2—minor falling danger).

Jump off the inside edge of the red flag ramp to the ramp that leads to the room above the Shotgun. These jumps help you to surprise people by taking routes they generally don't see. (2—falling danger).

Jump up from lower ramp to middle sniper tower platform—it's a good shortcut (2).

Jump from the courtyard to the cliff side ramp that leads to the Sniper Rife. Just make sure that you jump off to the left instead of directly to the top where the rifle is (3 falling danger).

Jump up from the middle sniper tower platform to the upper sniper platform (3—falling hazard).

Midship

Jump up onto the top ledge above the covering for one side of the top level (basically the highest point that you can get up) to get to the sniper perch that covers almost half the map (1).

Jump onto the middle gravity lift to get above the Shotgun (1—not very useful).

There is a crate in front of the blue base. You can jump from the crate in through the front window of the base if you crouch jump. It surprises lots of people when they see you do that (3).

Waterworks

Jump up crate to the top of the bases (1).

Jump from the Banshee room to the top of the base or the top of the Stationary Turret roof (2).

Crouch jump back from the top of the Stationary Turret to the Banshee room (3).

Jump off the sniper platform onto the ledge. Then you can run up the ledge and snipe from there. You are very exposed but nobody ever expects you there. (2 – this is a falling danger).

Zanzibar

Crouch or grenade jump up to the Battle Rifle in the alcove near Camp Froman (3).

Grenade jump onto top of wheelhouse tower (4).

Grenade jump onto ledge opposite wheelhouse tower—good for sniping (4).

Grenade jump from striped yellow windmill ledge (on the beach side) to the top of the wheelhouse tower (5).

Jump from the ledge at the bottom of the windmill up to the Rocket Launcher platform. This is a great shortcut but rather difficult (4).

Grenade jump onto top of the red base from the ledge above the stairs (5).

Grenade jump from the window shutters onto top of the red base (5).

And finally, my absolute favorite jump of the game: Jump from the rock—next to the Shotgun location—up to wheelhouse tower catwalk. During the initial rush you can surprise the defender by beating him to the top of the tower (3).

Chapter 9: Level Ranking System

Balance is a recurring theme in this Battle Guide and the Halo 2 ranking system is yet another example of a balancing act. Now that Halo 2 players have access to statistics and rankings, players understandably will be curious about how their ranks are determined. You can rest assured that Microsoft's Bungie team has put considerable effort into the level ranking system.

At face value, it may seem that collecting statistics and assigning a level ranking would be a facile task. However, you have to consider that the goal of this system is to be inclusive. A simple system might be fine for the players at the top of the heap, but what about everybody else out there who wants to play casual matchmaking games? The Halo 2 matchmaking system uses the level rankings to create well-balanced games for all classes of players. When you consider that a gamer's experience is enmeshed with the ranking system, then you can begin to understand the complexities of creating a level ranking system.

Not only must the ranking system be fair to players who excel, but it must also mitigate the burden of searching for people at one's own skill level. The ranking system must be able to differentiate between someone who plays well and someone who plays often. Without some creative tweaking, casual players would constantly find themselves playing against people above or below their own skill level.

The goal of this chapter is to give you an idea of how the Halo 2 ranking system is designed through the use of

> "Better learn balance... balance is key."
> — Mr. Miyagi, Karate Kid

hypothetic example. Many details of the Halo 2 ranking system have not yet been published; watch the Bungie website for articles on the subject. This chapter is a starting point. I trust that Microsoft will eventually publish excruciatingly verbose details about the level ranking system to satisfy.

Almost ELO

The first thing to understand about the Halo 2 ranking system is that it is loosely based on the ELO rating system. ELO was created to rank tournament chess players. The system assigns points for each win and ranks the players based upon the accumulation of these points. Once the players are ranked, it is relatively easy to extrapolate how many games each player should win against each ranked opponent. If the player performs better than expected, then his rank will increase. You can read all about ELO at http://en.wikipedia.org/wiki/ELO_rating_system.

> Although it is often written in capital letters, ELO is not an acronym. It is the surname of the system's creator Arpad Elo, a Hungarian-born physics professor.

One point of contention with using an ELO-like system is that it doesn't reward anything but the final result. When it comes to the Halo 2 ranking system, winning IS everything. This will be frustrating to players on the losing team who substantially outperform their teammates.

In addition, keep in mind that individual performance does not matter in team games, so there is absolutely no value to team killing. For example, if a player is rewarded for scoring a flag cap, then someone might be tempted to drop his teammate in order to get the point. I have seen someone shoot his teammate to get a point and I can write with 100% certainty that there is no benefit to this shameful behavior.

Matchmaking Playlists

Halo 2 rankings match players against opponents of similar skill level by using preset playlists. As you enter a Halo 2 online game, you choose which playlist you want to enter. These 'hoppers' include games such as 'Small Team' and they include both ranked and unranked playlists.

The Halo 2 Lobby.

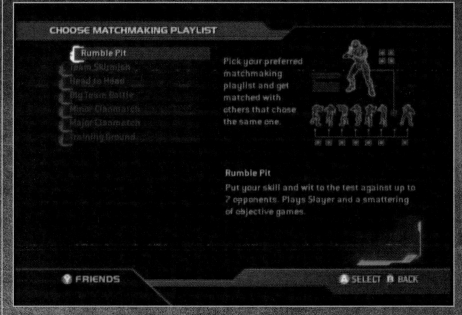

Sample Halo 2 playlists.

Players will only gain and lose points in the ranked playlists. For a casual player, this is great news. Once you have climbed to a level that you are comfortable with, you can simply switch to unranked hoppers. Although this will prevent you from climbing to a higher level, it will also allow you to stay at a constant level without worrying about your performance. In other words, you can play for fun.

Each ranked playlist has its own level ranking. For example, Armed could be at Level 10 in the Free For All (FFA) playlist but only Level 5 in the Small Team hopper. Without separate rankings, an elite FFA player would have to enter a team hopper against the top team players. This would be frustrating to those who choose to focus on some game types and play casually in other playlists. Your ranking for each level is available with your online statistics.

The Nitty Gritty

When it comes to climbing through the Halo 2 levels, your goal is very simple: win. If you win all of your games, then you will advance. Despite this simplicity, there are a few key principles of the ranking system:

- Each player's rank is based on his or her accumulated experience points.
- Players only gain or lose points in the ranked playlists.
- In team games, the winning team members gain points and the losing team members lose points.
- In FFA matches, you earn points for each player that you beat and you lose points for every player who beats you.
- Points are gained and lost based on the difference between players' levels.
- The rewards for winning are greater than the penalties for losing.

This section is purely a theoretical example of how a points system such as the Halo 2 ranking system works. These are not accurate examples; they are hypothetical cases to demonstrate how the model functions. In addition, the Halo 2 ranking system is maintained server-side so it is possible that the Bungie team can tweak it at any time.

To help illustrate these principles in action, imagine that Christa, Beth, Behr, and RNR are playing an FFA match. Christa is ranked at Level 10 in the FFA hopper. Beth is a Level 9 FFA player, Behr is a Level 8, and RNR is a Level 7.

The first thing that the ranking system calculates is the relative gain or loss for each level of variance. For example, let's say that players will gain 10 points each time they defeat another player with an equivalent level ranking. What point gain should Beth receive if she beats a higher ranked player such as Christa? If this one level of difference warrants a one point bonus, Beth will earn 11 points for defeating Christa. Conversely, if Christa defeats Beth, she will only earn nine experience points. Using these hypothetical numbers, we can construct the following table.

Points Earned for Each Level Difference

Level Difference	High Level Win	High Level Loss	Low Level Win	Low Level Loss
0	10	-10	10	-10
1	9	-10.5	11	-8.5
2	8	-11	12	-7
3	7	-11.5	13	-5.5
4	6	-12	14	-4

Based on these assumptions, you can calculate the net experience point totals for our players after their game.

Carnage Report for FFA Example Game

Name	Points	Kills	Deaths	Assists	Score
Behr (Level 8)	0	15	0	2	15
Christa (Level 10)	0	10	7	0	10
Beth (Level 9)	0	5	12	5	5
RNR (Level 7)	0	9	25	0	4

As you can see in the FFA Example Game chart, Behr had a great game and scored a total of 15 points. Because she defeated all of the other players, her results are the only ones that are all positive. The rest of the players will pay penalties for their losses.

Case in point, Behr (Level 8) managed to beat Christa (Level 10). Christa was ranked two levels above Behr, so Behr earns 12 points for defeating her. That is 10 points for the defeat plus 2 points for the level ranking differential. Behr also beat Beth (Level 9), who was one level above Behr, so Behr earns 11 points. RNR, however, was ranked one level below Behr, so Behr only receives 9 points for defeating him (10 points for the defeat minus 1 point for the level ranking differential). RNR clearly had a tough time with suicide penalties in our sample game.

Another factor in this system is that your point totals are altered based on the number of players in the match. This means that if your opponents are at the same level, playing a small team game can earn you roughly the same number of points as a large team game. In addition, keep in mind that it is possible to gain points but still lose the game. It all depends on the level of the other players.

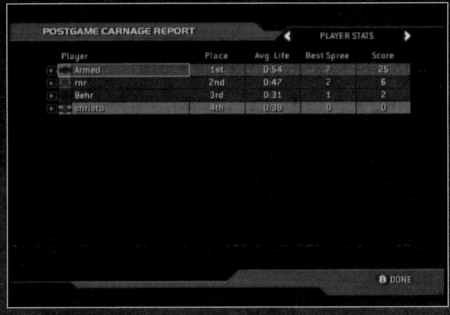

A sample Halo 2 Carnage Report.

Points Awarded to Each Player for FFA Example Game

Name	Result vs. Christa	Result vs. Beth	Result vs. RNR	Result vs. Behr	Net Points
Behr (Level 8)	12	11	9	N/A	+32
Christa (Level 10)	N/A	9	7	–11	+5
Beth (Level 9)	–8.5	N/A	8	–10.5	–11
RNR (Level 7)	–5.5	–7	N/A	–8.5	–21

This gives you an insight into the intricate workings of the Halo 2 level ranking system. However, we are not quite finished with the math portion of this guide. The astute reader may have already noticed that the Halo 2 system is not zero-sum. In other words, the reward for winning does not equal the penalty for losing. This results in an overall bias in the system. That bias is one of the balancing factors of the ranking. If the totals were zero-sum, it would be much more difficult for players to advance to higher levels—or maintain their rankings.

This is not the only mechanism in the system designed to mitigate the frustration associated with being stuck at a certain level. There is also a bonus built in to the system to allow lower level players to move up levels without as much friction as the elite players. This bonus is in the form of a multiplier. For example, a Level 5 player might have a 5% increase to his point total.

> The 'Points' column in our sample carnage report table is included for one simple reason: to stress once again that scoring points has no effect on your ranking. It does you no good to TK the flag carrier and get the cap!

Using the Stats from Bungie.net

For the deeply introspective gamer, the new Halo 2 online statistics are a dream come true. I seriously doubt that many people would ever consider gathering the type of data that Bungie is providing on their website. However, now that the data is freely available, I expect that people will find all sorts of uses for it.

For example, I was curious about my performance on different Halo 2 levels. I simply copied data from the recent games section and pasted it into a Microsoft Excel spreadsheet. After doing so, I quickly added headings and used the Freeze Panes feature to keep the headings visible. Then it was a simple matter of using an AutoFilter and sorting all of the results by the column of my choice. I admit that this may come across as being a little geeky, but it is also incredibly useful.

Based on these conveniently sorted statistics from Bungie.net, I found that I unequivocally sucked on the Lockout level, so I spent some time investigating the terrain and analyzing my play on that level. After a short time, I was able to bring my performance on Lockout up to par with the other levels. Using this same technique, you could potentially glean all sorts of insights into the facets of your gameplay. For example, you might want to know your average kills for each Halo 2 multiplayer map. To view your stats and a chart that shows how many experience points you need to get to the next level, visit http://bungie.net/stats/.

Level Ranking FAQ

Question: Do I get a bonus if I score a point (for example, planting a bomb or a flag cap)?

Answer: No.

Question: If I don't get a bonus for a flag cap, then why do I appear at the top of the carnage list?

Answer: Don't confuse the carnage report with the ranking system. The only thing that matters is winning. In team-based hoppers, all the other information is for your curiosity—the stats system doesn't care.

Question: But what if I get all the frags and all the caps but my team loses?

Answer: You lose.

Question: Do I get a bonus if my team is playing shorthanded?

Answer: No.

Question: Why is it so easy to drop a level down but so tough to get back up?

Answer: It may seem like it's easier to go down a level than it is to go up, but actually the opposite is true. The reason it seems this way is that you will immediately go up a level if you gain enough experience points to reach the next level. However, you will only drop a level once you have gone far below the points for the level below you. For example, if I were playing at Level 9, I would only drop to Level 8 after I had gone well below the Level 9 point total. Consequently, when I see my rank drop I am not on the line between Level 8 and 9, I have actually gone well below Level 9.

> "Winning isn't everything; it's the only thing."
> —Vince Lombardi

A SPARTAN running with the ball.

Chapter 10: Wort Wort Wort! Halo 2 Etiquette

The most important thing to remember about game etiquette is that the terms *etiquette* and *rule* are not synonymous. The game determines the rules of play; etiquette is an understanding between players. If you have not spoken to your fellow players about proper conduct, then you can't expect them to abide by your interpretation of Halo 2 etiquette. You should also be aware of common contentious behaviors so you can avoid being guilty of them. Once you have thought through these issues, you can decide with your friends which "gentleman's rules" you choose to adopt. If you are playing against strangers on Xbox *Live*™, don't expect them to adhere to any rules of etiquette.

The crux of the etiquette issue is that some of the things that people consider poor etiquette happen to be extremely effective techniques. In other words, the best offense is often offensive to others. I investigated the rules of some Xbox Halo 1 tournaments; none of the etiquette examples in this chapter were outlawed in any of the tournaments. In tournaments, the only banned behavior is exploiting bugs in the game (for example, backpack reloading or infinite ammo in Halo 1).

I'm sure that my friends and I will always have some understanding of our own player etiquette but keep in mind that this will not help your game. For example, when I played the Chill-Out level with my friends we had a gentleman's agreement that we wouldn't use the Rocket Launcher. This made the level more interesting for us but the downside was that I found myself at a disadvantage when I played against people who didn't abide by this rule. If I had been playing to win with my friends, I would have been better prepared for other games. If you want to be the best player that you can be, then play by tournament rules.

Camping

Of all the points of etiquette, camping is probably the most hotly disputed with practically every FPS game prompting arguments about the definition of term. *Camping* is staying in the same spot and waiting for unsuspecting victims to come by. Because the camper is often stationary, he won't always appear on the Halo 2 motion detector. The advantage is obvious—the camper will get the drop on anyone who comes along.

However, there is an awful lot of gray area when it comes to camping. How long does the camper have to be still before he is considered to be camping? How far does the camper have to move before he is considered to be in a different place? If you are running and you see that someone is coming around the corner, is it camping for you to stop and wait for him to come to you? If you asked a dozen Halo players these questions, they would probably give you a dozen different answers.

Try not to get worked up when you think that someone is camping. Since everyone has his or her own opinion about this topic, you may as well save yourself the aggravation and not let it get to you. Remember that people playing defense will almost certainly be camping. Personally, I don't like camping but it happens so I may as well get used to it.

Camping on a Lockout wall.

Spawn Camping

Spawn camping is camping by a spawn point or taking advantage of the spawn algorithm. For example, if you understand when players are likely to appear, you don't need to necessarily camp on the spawn spot. If you have line of sight, you could be across the map with a Sniper Rifle.

A newly spawned player will only have the default weapons, so a well-armed camper can almost certainly defeat a player who spawns before that person has a chance to fight back. Although some players consider this a lowly thing to do, Halo 1 tournaments did not outlaw it. In fact, as you have read in this book, it was a widely used lockdown strategy.

Spawn camping with a Scorpion on Waterworks.

Flag Tossing

The Halo 2 flag is heavy. If you are running with the flag, you will move slower than normal. One way to mitigate this is by *flag tossing*, which is to repeatedly pick up the flag and toss it forward. This allows you to move faster while still advancing the flag. Some people consider this technique to be bad manners and the folks at Bungie seem to agree. In Halo 2, there is an audio and visual indicator when the flag is dropped. In other words, this practice comes with a price. If you drop the flag, you will give away your position. However, if the other team already knows where the flag is located, flag tossing still has its advantages, so you should expect to see people doing it often despite being considered bad form.

Weapon Hoarding

Weapon hoarding is when one player is constantly taking weapons that he will not be able to use as effectively as his teammates. For example, one player should not take both the Sniper Rifle and the Rocket Launcher. By doing so, he has hindered his team. The players on the best teams will know exactly which weapons they should take and which they should leave for their teammates.

Crew 116 Tip: Weapon Hoarding

Not hoarding weapons is one of the marks of a good team. When playing clan games, we're good about calling which weapons we are going for and respecting people's roles.

—char

Leaving the Map

It's likely that someone will eventually find a way to get out of a Halo 2 map. If you're playing on a map with a known exploit, you'll want to determine whether leaving the map is acceptable before the game begins.

A Halo 1 example of this is the Ghost exploit on the Blood Gulch level. If you haven't seen this done in gameplay, do a search online and find the video. You'll see that it's possible to get right out of the map and back so far away that no one without a Sniper Rifle would be able to see you.

Leaving the Game

If you drop a game, the Halo 2 ranking system will not forget about you. In fact, if you do it on purpose, you will personally pay a penalty for bailing early. This is true regardless of when you decide to leave. If you ditch in the first few seconds, you will still take a point penalty. If you drop in an FFA match, you will automatically lose to everyone who finishes the game. The rest of your team will not take a direct penalty but they will be playing shorthanded.

Some people will doubtlessly figure out that when they drop a game that their team cannot lose it allows them to save time and still get the victory. (For example, when you're playing the last round of a CTF game and your team is up by two points.) However, you have to consider the fact that someone on your team must complete the game. If your entire team drops, then you will all lose. Don't leave your teammates in a shorthanded situation just because you're in a hurry to climb a level. After all, they might decide to leave at the same time and that means you will lose.

Parking Vehicles in Unusual Places

Parking a Ghost on the Zanzibar beach flag spot is common. This technique is effective because one can't simply run up with the flag; even a glancing blow from a vehicle can kill the flag carrier. This forces the offense to move the ghost before they can score. Some people argued that this was a cheap trick, but others believe that this is just a good strategy.

Since vehicles are now destructible, this may not be as big of an issue for Halo 2. For example, there may not be an opportunity as effective as parking a Scorpion on a Halo 1 Blood Gulch flag spot.

I have read that some Halo PC tournaments banned parking vehicles inside bases. However, I haven't read about any Xbox tournaments using this rule. Until you are told otherwise, park wherever you want.

Guarding the Zanzibar flag spot with a Ghost.

Screen Cheating

Screen cheating is when a player looks at an opponent's screen; however, not everyone shares this view (pardon the pun). If you are playing with someone on the same box and you don't want him to look at your screen, ask him not to do so. Just keep in mind that it's very easy to see things like colors and explosions even if you aren't intentionally looking at the other person's screen space. If you find that you are arguing with your buddies about this, just bite the bullet and throw out the rule. It's not worth the hassle and it's impossible to enforce.

Karaoke Wannabes

Although this isn't a Halo 2-specific issue, it is a common enough practice that it warrants a mention. Nobody should complain about the odd bit of useless banter and good-natured taunting, but using the mike just to annoy people is bad etiquette no matter what game you're playing. There is a difference between psychological warfare and acting like an idiot.

When you run into those yahoos out there that sing into the mike or just make fools of themselves, just ignore them. In a game like Halo 2 where good communication plays a vital role in the overall success, this kind of behavior is definitely bad etiquette.

Strong Silent Types

Equally as annoying as singing throughout the game are the strong silent types. Now I can understand not communicating with your teammates if you've broken your communicator or the cat has chewed through the wires. However, if that's not the case, it's bad form not to communicate with your teammates. Communication plays a large role in the success of your team. If someone is employing Spawn camping to keep your team from getting out of your Spawn point, speak up! Let your teammates know so they can help out and rid your spawn of that nefarious wretch. If you're going for the flag, let your teammates know so they can back you up or give you cover. Just like in any sport, good communication and discussion of your team strategy will go a long way toward your team's overall success. Team games are for team players; if you're not interested in teams, then play FFA (Free For All).

Poaching

This one is a bit of a stretch, but in the interest of completeness, it should be addressed. A player is *poaching* when he intentionally stays out of battles so he can steal one shot kills without risking a fight. It's tough to argue that a player is poaching because after all, who wouldn't want their teammate to finish off someone that they have engaged? Personally, I wouldn't worry much about this breach of etiquette. It is difficult to prove that it is occurring, so it is rarely worth your objections.

Poaching on Ivory Tower.

Teamwork in FFA Games

Free For All (FFA) is not a team game. It is inappropriate for you to join an FFA game and work with other players. If you want to play a team game, then you should enter a team game. You should not try to change the rules of an FFA game. This type of behavior will make you very unpopular, especially if the other players recognize what is happening during the game.

Team Killers and Griefers

Griefers are people who annoy their own team. Essentially, griefers do things that make it more difficult for the team to accomplish its goal. For example, a griefer might take one of the team's vehicles and purposely drive it around aimlessly, depriving the team of a valuable resource.

The worst form of griefer is the *team killer* (TKer). TKers are players who intentionally kill their own teammates, and this practice is always exceptionally poor form. I've seen people kill the flag carrier on the Zanzibar beach so they can score the point. Remember that there is absolutely no advantage—in the stats system or otherwise—to killing your

teammate. You will not get a personal bonus if you plant the bomb or capture the flag—all that matters is that your team wins. If you go after your own teammates, all you will do is annoy your teammates, have a longer spawn time, and probably get booted from the game. Halo 2 has been enhanced to avoid team killing. Your teammates are harder to kill than your opponents.

Note that players will occasionally down their teammates accidentally, which is known as a 'betrayal'. Although this is just part of the game, you should strive to be charged with as few betrayals as possible.

I expect that a registry of TKers will appear at some point. If you get onto this list, good luck finding a good game. Do not be a TKer!

Team killing...don't do it.

Appendix A: Halo 2 Glossary

Add. Occurs when players unexpectedly join a fight. The term comes from Massively Multiplayer Online Role-Playing Games (MMORPGs). For example, if two players are in the middle of a fight, another player might 'add' into the battle.

Brick. A player who is underperforming; a drag on the team.

Cloth. Slang for the Halo flag.

Cap. Short for 'capture'. When playing Capture the Flag, a 'cap' is a point.

Camper. A player who stays in the same area for a long period of time.

Covenant Fusion Core. A discarded Covenant energy source. Fusion cores are highly explosive.

Covenant Fusion Cores.

CTF (Capture the Flag). A multiplayer game type in which teams must steal a flag and return it to their base.

Dual Wielding. Carrying a weapon in each hand; also known as DW.

Elite. A powerful Covenant race. Elites are not as large as Brutes or Hunters but they are agile and carry weapons such as the deadly Plasma Sword. The Elite is always one of the two playable models in multiplayer Halo 2 games.

Feint. A military tactic of deception that obscures a player's intention. For example, a player may make a feint by attacking with a Magnum and holding a Plasma Sword in reserve. When the opponent believes that he will score an easy victory, he moves in close enough for the wily player to swipe him with the Plasma Sword.

FFA (Free For All). A game type in which all players battle each other. Also known as a 'deathmatch.'

FFA Slayer. An FFA match in which players score points by defeating other players.

Flag Tossing. This occurs when a player intentionally drops a flag that he is carrying. Players do this because one cannot run quickly while carrying the flag.

Flanking. A military maneuver that involves exposing a weak side of the 'flanked' opponent. For example, a player might maneuver so that he is firing at the back of another player.

FPS (First Person Shooter). A game type, such as Halo 2, that features a first person perspective of a shootout.

Frag. Slang for an FPS (First Person Shooter) kill.

Glassing. The Covenant practice of annihilating a planet by melting the surface into glass.

Griefer. A jerk who intentionally annoys his own team.

The Guardians. When the Halo 2 engine does not understand why a player died, the game displays the message "You were killed by the guardians."

Hog. Slang term for the Warthog Light Reconnaissance Vehicle.

Hopper. Slang term for a Halo 2 matchmaking playlist.

HUD (Heads Up Display). The Halo 2 HUD displays onscreen details such as your shield status and your motion tracker.

Hunter. A large Covenant race. Hunters travel in pairs referred to as 'bonded pairs.' Hunters are vulnerable in the orange parts of their body (for example, the small of their backs).

Invis. Slang term for invisibility; refers to the Active Camouflage powerup.

KotH (King of the Hill). A Halo game type in which players try to occupy a certain part of the map for a designated period of time.

Level. Level can refer to either a multiplayer map, or an Xbox *Live*™ skill level.

Lockdown. Getting control of the other team; this usually implies that the other team is being taken out near their spawn spots.

LPB (Low Ping Bastard). Someone who has a fast connection and often gets chosen as the host. In network games, the host has an advantage because his Xbox does not have to wait for updates that come across the wire. This means that he sees everything right when it happens; other players may experience a small delay.

Melee. Punching an opponent with your weapon. A melee to the back of the head will take down most of your enemies.

MJOLNIR. A special form of body armor that only SPARTANs can wear. The armor features a rechargeable energy shield and is named for the hammer carried by Thor, the Norse God of Thunder.

Nade. Slang term for grenade.

Noob. Slang term for a beginner player. The term is derived from the popular term 'Newbie.'

ODST (Orbital Drop Shock Trooper). Elite human troops trained to make extremely hazardous drops from orbit.

Overshield. A Halo 2 powerup that temporarily increases a player's shield strength.

Pincushion. A player who has been filled with Covenant needle shards.

Pineapple. Slang for a Fragmentation Grenade.

Playing Possum. Pretending to be in a weak position to entice your opponent to engage. For example, firing an SMG at a vehicle and then pulling out the Rocket Launcher when the vehicle approaches. Also known as a 'bait and switch' ambush.

Poaching. Occurs when a player stays away from a battle and hopes to score the fatal shot.

Powerup. One of the Halo 2 goodies that give players an advantage. Powerups include the Overshield, which makes a player's shields stronger than usual and the Active Camouflage that renders the player almost invisible.

Puma. Slang term for the Warthog. This term comes from the online Halo fan Red Vs. Blue© movies (www.redvsblue.com).

Ranking System. Halo 2 has an online ranking system that matches players of similar skill levels.

Reticle. The onscreen targeting sight of your weapon.

Screen Cheating. Looking at another player's screen to figure out where the player is located.

Shottie. Slang term for the Shotgun.

Slayer. A multiplayer game type based on points for kills.

Sneak. A player who is given the duty of covert movement and reconnaissance.

SPANKr. Slang for the Halo rocket launcher; pronounced 'spanker.' Take a close look at the side of the launcher to see this name on it.

The effects of a good pineapple toss.

SPARTAN. A group of humans selected during their childhood to be made into super soldiers. SPARTANs undergo extensive training and physical alterations to enhance their abilities. The Master Chief was a result of the SPARTAN-II project.

Spawn Algorithm. The logic used to determine where and when a player spawns.

Spawn Camping. Staying near a spawn point in an attempt to engage players who haven't had the chance to acquire weapons that are better than the defaults.

Strafe. Running to the side. Used commonly for dodging and aiming.

Team Killer (TKer). Someone who intentionally kills his teammates.

Team Slayer. A team version of the 'Slayer' game type. See *Slayer*.

Weapon Hoarding. Preventing proper weapon allocation during team games.

Wort Wort Wort! This is an insult that the Covenant Elites used during the Halo 1 campaign. Basically, it's alien trash talk.

> "Game over man, it's game over."
> —Private Hudson, *Aliens*

Index

X

Xbox Live

  network, 3

  roles in, 85

  rounds in, 85

Z

Zanzibar, 178–183

  advice on, 179, 182

  main gate, opening, 69

  strategy for, 182–183

  trick jumps in, 185

  weapons for, 181

zero-sum totals, 191

zone defense, 99

  weapons allocation and, 84